THEATRE

David Mamet is a director and the author of numerous acclaimed plays, books, and screenplays. His play *Glengarry Glen Ross* won the Pulitzer Prize, and his screenplay for *The Verdict* was nominated for an Academy Award. He lives in Santa Monica, California.

THEATRE

DAVID MAMET

faber and faber

First published in the US by Faber Inc in 2010
First published in the UK in 2010
by Faber and Faber Limited
Bloomsbury House, 74–77 Great Russell Street,
London WC1B 3DA

Printed in England by CPI Mackays, Chatham

A CIP record for this book
is available from the British Library

ISBN 978–0–571–25524–5

2 4 6 8 10 9 7 5 3 1

This book is dedicated to Linda Kimbrough

The arena, the card-table, the magic circle, the temple, the stage, the screen, the tennis court, the court of justice, etc., are all in form and function play-grounds, i.e., forbidden spots, isolated, hedged round, hallowed, within which special rules obtain. All are temporary worlds within the ordinary world, dedicated to the performance of an act apart.

—Johan Huizinga, *Homo Ludens*

CONTENTS

Contents

THEATRE

INTRODUCTION

I read a lot of technical material about the theatre when I was young.

The Neighborhood Playhouse distributed a reading list to its students in 1967, and we were supposed to have read the forty or fifty titles before the first day of class.

The books, as I recall, were predominantly Russian—Stanislavsky's trilogy (*An Actor Prepares*, *Building a Character*, and *Creating a Role*) and *My Life in Art*; Nemirovich-Danchenko (his partner in the Moscow Art Theatre) writing about Stanislavsky; Nikolai Gorchakov's *Stanislavsky Directs* and his *The Vakhtangov School of Stage Art*.

Books by and about the Moscow Art Theatre's second generation, the studios, filled out the list. In addition to the thought of Vakhtangov, we were exposed to that of Meyerhold (his rival, the pretender to the throne).

After the generation of the studios (Meyerhold and Vakhtangov), the locus of succession shifted to their Muscovite disciples in New York and their work. We read Stella Adler, Harold Clurman, Robert Lewis (*Method or Madness*), and so on.

I gobbled this stuff up. I was a rotten actor and a hopeless acting student, but I loved the theatre and I loved the theoretical, and I delighted in tracing the vein of Muscovite thought through the apostolic succession.

For that succession extended down to me.

The head of my school, my teacher, was Sanford Meisner, baby of the Group Theatre. He came of age with the Adlers, Morris Carnovsky, Lee Strasberg, Harold Clurman, and the host of technophiles.

(Clurman and Stella Adler had made a pilgrimage to Paris to meet with Stanislavsky in the thirties and had received the laying on of hands. Was I not a student of their colleague? Yes, I was. And I am proud to have known and studied with Mr. Meisner, to have socialized with Harold Clurman, Stella Adler, and Bobby Lewis.

I admired their accomplishments and pored over their books; but, on reflection, I had (and have) little idea what they were talking about.

I exempt Harold Clurman, who age eighty or so took my wife to the theatre. Halfway through the first act she felt his hand on her knee and gliding up her skirt. "Harold, *please*," she said. "What are you *doing*?" And he replied, "I come to the theatre to enjoy myself."

Well, so do I, and so do we all; and that's the only reason we come or should come.

We should not come, whether as workers or audience, to practice or share a "technique." There is no such thing as a "Stanislavsky actor" or a "Meisner actor" or a "Method actor." There are actors (of varying abilities) and nonactors.

The job of the actor is to perform the play such that his performance is more enjoyable—to the audience—than a mere reading of the text.

Similarly, the job of the designers of costumes, sets, and lights, is to increase the audience's enjoyment of the play past that which might be expected in a performance done in street clothes, on a bare stage, under work lights.

This is a very difficult task indeed, for most plays are better enjoyed under such circumstances, as anyone who has ever seen a great rehearsal in a rehearsal hall can attest.

Why is this great rehearsal more enjoyable than the vast bulk of designed productions? It allows the audience to use its imagination, which is the purpose of coming to the theatre in the first place.

It takes a real artist to increase the enjoyment of

the audience past that which would be found in seeing the play on a bare stage, for the first rule of the designer, as of the physician, is do no harm. And, as with the physician, the rule is quite often observed in the breach.

What of the director?

Actors, left alone, will generally stage the play better than it could be staged by all but a few directors.

Why?

Actors never forget that which most directors never realize: The purpose of staging is to draw the attention of the audience to the person speaking.

Each actor in the directorless play will insist (for his own reasons) on being seen, heard, and rationally featured for that portion of the play in which the playwright has indicated he should be the center of attention.

Further, the actors, thinking, as they should, that the most interesting parts of the play are those which feature themselves, will, in committee, vote to get *on* with it, and move this play along.* Which is all the audience cares about.

---

*If you think about it, this desire of the actor to get to the part where *he* talks and the desire of the character to do the same are indistinguishable to the audience—if we say, as I will later, that there is no such thing as the character, then these two urges are not merely indistinguishable, but identical.

Introduction

The task of the good director, then, is to focus the attention of the audience through the arrangement of the actors, and through the pace and rhythm of the presentation.

And there you have it. Actor, designers, director. First and last, their job is to bring the play to the audience. Any true technique, then, would consist—and consist solely—in a habitual application of those ideas that will aid in so doing.

"But," the observant may remark, "did not the Moscow Art Theatre, its studios, the Group, et cetera, did they not, irrespective of their adoration of the theoretical, do good and even great work? And has not the author himself and at length, offered the world theoretical treatises?" It is all true; and I suggest that such treatises and theories be accepted not as instruction manuals but as the otherwise incathectable expression of love for an ever-widening mystery, in which spirit I offer these essays.

THE GREENROOM

The greenroom is that common room between the street and the stage. In coming backstage, one enters the greenroom first. I've heard, over the years, several derivations of the term: The original room was painted green, or was constructed by a man named Green. None are convincing.

Early nineteenth-century British novels refer to the greenroom in a country house. They mean by this that transitional space known in New England as the mudroom. This mudroom in old farmhouses (including my own) allowed the farmer, hunter, outdoorsman to divest himself of those accoutrements that were needed on the land but inappropriate in the house. Mine, in Vermont, was filled, according to the seasons, with fishing rods, snowshoes, muddy boots, firearms, longbows, skis, skates, a snow shovel, a maul, the walls covered with hooks bearing all sorts of coats and caps, and on the floor a wooden drying rack covered with gloves, gaiters, sweaters.

The Greenroom

In Vermont, the mudroom; in England, the green-room, where one knocked off the grass, grain, and green of the field. On the farm, the greenroom was the space between the farm and the home; in the theatre, it rests between the sacred and the profane.

Many of the observations and suggestions in this book might be considered heretical.

That is, if the theatre were a religion. But, though its origins are linked with religion, the theatre as an art is a profession, and, in its appearance as show business, is something of a racket.

This book is a compilation and a distillation of those thoughts and attendant practices I have used in my forty years in the professional theatre. They are the rules by which I function as an artist and by which I have been able to make a living.

Faced with a difficult medical decision, we are most comforted to hear the physician endorse one of the choices by saying, "This is what I would do if it were my *own* child."

The ideas herein, similarly, are what I would (and do) tell my own children and my students. I will gladly test their practicality and practicability against anyone willing to put his particular philosophy to a practical test.

Of what might such a test consist? The ability to motivate an actor to perform an action simply and unself-consciously; to involve an audience; and, at a somewhat more abstract level, to communicate a directorial or literary vision to a designer such that his designs will serve the show.

Finally, I am suggesting and describing a way of *thinking* about the drama (analysis) and of *communicating* the subsequent conclusions using language and vocabulary (direction).

Impracticable theory is an impediment to both art and sustenance, and benefits no one save the intellectual to whom theatrical thought is an abstract and enjoyable exercise. But the point of the theatre is to give the *audience* enjoyment, and it is my experience that to do so, the practitioner is going to have to learn discipline.

This is primarily a discipline of *thought* and *speech*. Its overriding principle is never to consider or to suggest that which is impossible to accomplish.

As a young student I abhorred direction and instruction that was incapable of being done. I still do. It called for a collusion between the student and the teacher-director: "I will pretend to an approximation of what I think you want if you will refrain from criticizing me."

The theatre does not need more teachers or more directors; it needs more writers and actors, and both come from the same applicant pool: those who are affronted, bemused, fascinated, or saddened by the infinite variety of human interaction, which always bodes so promising and usually ends so ill.

This applicant pool is interested in the truth, and they love to act and write.

Here follow certain thoughts about these people and the audience that craves their productions.

THE HUNTER AND THE GAME

Game does not disappear because of overhunting but because of destruction of habitat. It takes one hundred square miles to support a grizzly bear and hundreds of acres to support a herd of deer.

In the theatre, the habitat in which the artist must flourish is the audience.

In 1967, when I was in acting school in New York, there were seventy-two new Broadway plays produced. In 2009 there were forty-three, of which half were revivals.

Why the diminution? The habitat has disappeared—the audience, which is to say, the middle class, is gone.

They were the arbiters of American theatre, for American theatre would reach the hinterlands only via Broadway, and the Broadway play would fail or succeed upon its ability to appeal to the middle class. One might say that the true arbiters were the critics, but this only places the correct answer at one remove, for the critics, then as now, served, whether they know it or not, at the pleasure of the paper's advertisers, which is to say, at the pleasure of the consumers, which is to say, the audience.

This Broadway audience, which supported the plays of O'Neill, Odets, Saroyan, Wilder, Miller, and Williams, was educated or, in any case, literate, middle-class, largely Jewish. They enjoyed discussion and those plays that fostered discussion, for most in their community saw the plays.

No more. Today's Broadway audience is predominantly tourists and the wealthy vacationers who, in the main, are the only ones who can afford life in New York. These may be tourists full stop, or that genus the rural Vermonters of my youth referred to as "the year-round summer people," that is to say, those who cannot fully participate in the community, as they need not rely upon one another.

These current New Yorkers do not participate in the day-to-day life of the world in which they are domiciled, or do so at a much lower level than those middle-class New Yorkers of old; as they do not participate, that communal interaction that gives rise both to the audience and to the playwrights does not occur. I wrote a new play last year and asked my New York producer if he didn't think that it would, perhaps, fare better off rather than on Broadway, and he gave me a rueful smile and explained, "There *is* no off-Broadway," and further, that there had not been for twenty years.

There is only Broadway. There are fewer theatres. More than 25 percent of off-off Broadway theatres have closed in the last five years alone, mostly in Midtown and the West Village.

The worth of Midtown real estate has raised the rents of the Broadway theatres, and, for an average play to recoup its investment, it must run fifteen weeks at near capacity. Which is to say, it must fill 1,200 seats, at an average ticket price of $77.

To whom, then, must this play appeal? To risk $11 million, the play, to the rational investor, must be odds-on to appeal to the tourist.

The tourist has no memory of last year's play and actors, he does not come to see the new work of a director, of a playwright, or of a designer. He comes to see a *spectacle*, which will neither provoke nor disturb, whose worth cannot be questioned. He does not come with the theatrical curiosity of the native theatregoer but with the desire for amusement, and he comes as to an amusement park, for the thrill first of experiencing, and next, and perhaps more important, of being able to relate *having experienced* that particular thrill deprived to the stay-at-homes. He wants to brag of having seen star X or star Y. The tourist goes to the theatre much as I went, in London, to see the Crown Jewels.

No adult Londoner would go to see the Crown Jewels, and no adult New Yorker went to see *Mamma Mia!* for to do so would have been culturally repugnant, branding him as a tourist or dufus.

New York, with the rise in real estate prices and the disappearance of manufacture, business, and, thus, of the middle class, has become New York Land.

What of the critics?

The readership of *The New York Times* is the wealthy, in effect, the *rentier*, which is to say, he who has *got* to where he was going, and our paper of record, absent a constituency of the theatrically savvy, has become a champion of the moot, appealing to the intellectual pretensions of its readership.

The paper, de facto cultural censor, writes (I will not say "panders") to the intellectually pretentious—"You must experience the *meaning* of this play"—while it also pushes the transient—"Thrills, chills, and an exploding set. KILL to get a ticket!!!"

The currency of any new play depends on its reception in New York. If it is not staged in New York, it will not be printed or awake the interest of the stock and amateur theatres from which a playwright might derive continued income. If it is not well received in New York, it will fare similarly. And that is the news from Lake Wobegon: The habitat has disappeared.

Now, the desire for drama has not disappeared, and

one may find it gratified through various new venues, electronic and, as always, local and jury-rigged. Though there is much less chance of these local efforts migrating to Gotham and thence to the world, there is increased possibility of them finding a wider audience on the Internet. And so it goes.*

---

*It would be as pointless today to decry the disappearance of the New York stage for a previous generation as to lament the demise of radio drama. The young of today will have their own "good old days."

HUNTING INSTINCTS

Man is never happier than when he is going hunting.

—José Ortega y Gasset

Man is a predator. We know this because our eyes are in the front of our heads. The same conclusion may be reached by reading the newspapers.

As predators we close out the day around the camp-fire with stories of the hunt.

These stories, like the chase itself, engage our most primal instinct of pursuit:* The story's hero is in pursuit of his goal—the hiding place of the stag or the cause of the plague on Thebes or the question of Desdemona's chastity or the location of Godot.

In the hunt story, the audience is placed in the same position as the protagonist: The viewer is told

---

*That is why our eyes are found in front—to aid pursuit. Prey animals' eyes are found on the side, to search for predators.

what the goal is and, like the hero, works to determine what is the best thing to do next—he wonders what happens next. How may he determine what is the best course toward the goal? Through observation. He, the viewer, watches the behavior of the hero and his antagonists, and guesses what will happen next. This is the essence of the story around the campfire: "And you'll never guess what happened next . . ."

In this prognostication we engage the same portion of the brain that we use in the hunt: the ability to spontaneously process and act upon information without subjecting the process to verbal (conscious) review.

This is the apparent paradox of dramatic writing. It is not, though it may appear to be, the communication of ideas but rather the inculcation in the audience of the instincts of the hunt. These instincts precede and, in times of stress, supersede the verbal; they are spontaneous and more powerful than the assimilation of an idea.

The mere presentation of an idea is called a lecture. A lecture induces in the listener that ruminative state necessary for comparison and evaluation of ideas. This is the usual state of the civilized being—a dampening of the predatory instincts in order to allow communal cooperation.

This is all well and good, but it is not the stuff of drama, which, by fulfilling a more basic need—to exercise our most primal instincts—has the power not only to please but also, curiously, to unite. For the audience, when moved, is moved on a preverbal level. It is not involved in sharing the *ideas* of the drama, but rather experiences the thrill of the communal hunt. This suspension of the analytical faculty is also experienced in the falling-in-love portion of mating, in gambling, in combat, in sport.

When we rise from the drama we resume our intellectual pretensions and ascribe our enjoyment to our ability to appreciate its engaging themes and ideas. This (like the societal election of the newspaper critic as censor) is an attempt to regain autonomy.

But we are not actually moved by the ideas in plays, nor, primarily, even by the presence of poetry. We appreciate plays in translation, and what do we know of the Russian of Chekhov? And we have argued for four hundred years about the "meaning" of *Hamlet*.

Certainly a play, being not only a celebration of the hunt but a hunt itself, will benefit from an author's genius as a poet—Shakespeare was the greatest poet in the English language. But the second-greatest was Yeats, and he couldn't write a play to save his soul. Poetry is insufficient; beauty in language itself (see again, Chekhov in translation) is nonessential. What is essential? The plot.

The critical and academic love of issue plays reveals

a misunderstanding of drama. It is the civilized man's misunderstanding, which is to say, a misappreciation of the power of his own reason. "We are all here together in this theatre; therefore, let's use our time wisely and listen to a lecture whose meaning may be encapsulated and so taken home with us."

But this lecture has no power to unite. For as much as we hail the correct proclamation of the apparent truth, we, the audience, have had no experience together. We, the audience, were merely stuck at a lecture.

But the drama is, essentially, people stuck in an elevator.

Those of us who have been in similar extremity cherish the experience the rest of our lives, for as trying and inconvenient as it was at the time, we remember the unity of communal endeavor and value this cessation of our mundane worries. It was cleansing to experience that we could put aside the so pressing activities of the day and find that the world went on in any case, while our new, small tribe searched for a solution to its communal problem.

The hours in the elevator, the hours in the theatre, are the communal hunt for a solution. As such, the experiences are indelible, for they engage not the consciousness but also a different order and more effective part of the brain.

Hunting Instincts

The soldier, the gambler, the fighter need to be shown something only once. They do not need to be convinced by explanation. Shown something that will cost or save their lives, they will remember it. Their actual brain waves have been changed, because their life depends on it. They, here, are the predator animal.

But the passivity during the lecture and issue play is the reaction of the prey animal: Sit still and listen while you are told something you already know and are charged for it. Do not fear, for nothing will excite you.

But we use a different part of our brain to actually appreciate drama. We civilized folk use it seldom and we love to exercise it. Go into a theatre and feel the audience enthralled in a play. One can feel it backstage, and with one's eyes closed—a physiologic change is taking place through communal absorption in the hunt.*

It is the excitation of the hunting instinct that accounts for the special pleasure we take in drama. (The storyteller around the campfire excites our vicari-

*Compare the casino. It will hold, that is, keep, 18 percent of every dollar wagered. It is thus unreasonable to assume anything other than that a gambler will lose 18 percent of his wagers. But it is enjoyable to pit oneself against the Fates, which is the essence of casino gambling, and it is for this experience that the gambler pays. Note also that we watch a majority of marriages end in acrimony and yet, in love, it is impossible to feel anything other than that one's particular engagement will be the exception. Knowing the "odds," falling in love is nonetheless enjoyable, as, indeed, a gift from the gods.

ous participation in the near miss with the bear, but the viewer is in no actual danger of mauling.)

Let us note that suspension of disbelief does not mean we accept the implausible but rather we suspend the rational process of intellectualization, which is to say, of the comparison of phenomenon to idea, which is a process too slow to be of use in the hunt.

The suspension of disbelief is better characterized as a suspension of reason and, as such, can be seen as an essentially religious action—a surrender in the face of the gods or Fates, and a confession that our prized reason, and so our humanity, is fundamentally flawed and that we are sinners, torn between evil and good, between consciousness and passion, and deluded in our assessment of our own powers.

In this hunt, our self-confidence is at last revealed as arrogance, our reason as folly, and, by being brought low, we are cleansed—just as in the confessional, or on Yom Kippur, or in any true apology.

This is the story of the hunt, the war story, the story around the campfire. It is always a confession of the powerlessness of man over the intentions of the gods— in these we fail the easiest of tasks and succeed in the most impossible of endeavors, as the Fates will.

As predators we understand our entire life, and each discrete section of it (the day, the week, youth, maturity, age, the new job) as a hunt.

Hunting Instincts

We hunt for security, fame, happiness, compensation, et cetera. Psychiatry is an attempt to bring to the conscious mind the nature of the hunt and, so, reason backward to the underlying needs of the sufferer—to bring to consciousness the unconscious assumptions and goals whose incompatibility with possibility are making the analysand unhappy.

Drama is not an attempt on the part of the dramatist to clarify but rather to present, in its unfiltered, disturbing form, the hunt of the individual (the protagonist) such that, in its perfect form (tragedy), the end of the play reveals the folly of the hero's (and so the audience's) assumptions about the world and himself.

THE LAMPPOST AND
THE ALLEY

A cop's walking his beat one night. He discovers a drunk, on his hands and knees, crawling around near a lamppost.

"What are you doing?" asks the cop.

"I'm looking for my car keys," the drunk says. "I lost 'em in the alley."

"If you lost 'em in the alley," the cop says, "why are you looking for them *here*?"

The drunk says, "Light's better here."

It's easy to write issue plays, for it is easy to rile people up. The last few national elections have seen the country virtually split in half in rancor, the right thinking the left fools and the left thinking the right monsters.

Being members of a democracy, we not only "care" but also enjoy as our right "caring." There is no lack of things to care about—the environment, race, poverty, religion, abortion, homosexuality, marriage, illness, government, and so on. How wonderful.

The Lamppost and the Alley

The theatre has become vastly political in my lifetime. Where once we had "weepers," matinee structures featuring women abandoned, impregnated, deserted by their children or spouse, and so on—survival of the Victorian sensation novel, in the sixties we began to see this love of melodrama recast as politics—giving the weeping audience not only the pleasure of a good cry, but also a pat on the back for knowing that group X were people too.

All right. The villain always has a waxed mustache, or can be counted on to stand for social positions that have vanished from our country everywhere but on the stage. Old Style:

"You must pay the rent."

"I *can't* pay the rent."

New Style:

"You weak and unacceptable woman, homosexual, African American, go away, I do not want you."

"But, does no one see that we are people *too* . . . ?"

Same thing.

It is easy to write this play, as the course of events is known, and one may simply paint in the spaces according to the predrawn pattern. (Does anyone remember the paint-by-numbers phenomenon of the fifties? Does it still exist? One got a canvas presketched, with the shadings of each section numbered, the numbers corresponding to those on the tubes of paint included in the set.)

But the light is *not* good in the alley.

And the alley is the dark, hidden, forbidden human soul.

The light is not better there. There is no light, and a trip down into that alley, for the writer or actor, may be disturbing, revolting, frightening, for that is where the monster of our self lives, and there we may find not only the falsity of our constructed personality but also the truth of our feverishly suppressed perceptions.

The dark alley lies beyond the rational and, so, beyond the conscious. To face the notions there, to entertain them, is dangerous. For how may we value them? Are they the thoughts of madness? Will they be acceptable to the public? Are they acceptable to the artist? They may not be plotted upon a previously existing and accepted graph of values.

In this the journey down this alley differs from the issue play, again, for one may, in writing a play suggesting that X are people too, foresee or predict at least some acceptance, if not for the play, at least for the notion. But how do we value the fact that Nora leaves home; or that Estragon and Vladimir are left, at the end of the play, in the same state in which we found them at the beginning; or how to value that the mother in

The Lamppost and the Alley

Doubt pleads with the nun to allow her son to have a homosexual relationship with his teacher?

It is dark in the alley because we have removed the light from those things we would much rather not examine. But the desire to examine them, to bring them to light, to form the unformed thoughts into a logical presentation, is the desire to create art. And the repressive mechanism, just as it darkens the alley, also illuminates the worthless. See almost all modern poetry in our contemporary magazines. I suggest this test: Quote one line. One cannot.

And yet one might quote much of Yeats or Shakespeare, having read it once and long ago.

Who is the "drunk"? He is you and me. He is in an altered state, and he has gone there of his own volition. That is the meaning of his drunkenness. He has made himself drunk as his reason has failed him. He *confronts* the repressive mechanism, his true antagonist. The repressive mechanism is, of course, the cop, who, in his inebriation, the drunk mistakes for a helper, and from whom the cop asks for and receives the truth. The joke seems to concern the drunk and the keys—but the *drama* concerns the drunk and the cop. Hell of a joke.

THE FATAL SPIN

Early pilots knew that a spin was fatal, for no pilot had ever survived a spin.

But with the increased use of parachutes, a pilot who had left the plane and parachuted to the ground often saw the now pilotless plane right itself—that is, the plane, left alone, would self-correct out of a spin— leading the aeronautic community to deduce that a spin was survivable, if one could learn from the natural reactions of the plane. The plane was not causing the spin; the *pilot* was.

Having accepted as gospel that a spin was uncorrectable, any further investigation was not to be forthcoming. But the opposite assumption yielded the simple true answer.

If we assume that all plays need an intellectual director and a tricked-out set, we are blind to the actual operations of the theatrical transaction.

If we assume that they do not, that the play and the

actors can "fly themselves," as it were, and observe that interaction with the audience, we may learn something about how the mechanism (the play and the theatrical interchange) actually operates. Let us assume that we have no clue, and that, with a theatrical impulse in our hearts, we show-offs, class clowns, smart alecks, and so on, you and I, in short, have left the plane. But the plane flies on. We see plays without a director, self-directed by the amateur, summer stock, school, backyard group, doing just fine. What use, then, were the dramaturges, whatever they may do: the directors, the teachers, the interpreters, and the intellectuals who wish, through manipulation of the set, lights, or text, to impart "meaning" to that which, they would have us believe, would have no meaning prior to their shenanigans? Of little or no use at all. The play will fly itself.

We have all said, "I saw it on Broadway, and I saw the production at the local Elks, and, do you know, the Elks was better!" What does this mean? That we enjoyed the play *and* that we were thrilled not to be messed around by a bunch of ideologues who claimed to be pulling the wagon but were, instead, prancing ahead with a baton.

We all put on plays.

The seduction, proposal, proposition, family fight, resignation, plea for a raise—these are all dramas, with protagonists (ourselves) and antagonists (the other). They contain beginnings, closings, set pieces, and are steeped in our love of comedy and tragedy, the grand, often misunderstood nonetheless noble drama of our own grand and tragic lives.

What do we need to put these on the stage? A text and some actors.

Will success attract directors, producers, critics, dramaturges, professors, teachers, and so on? Of course. California in 1849 attracted goldbugs. But we should note that those who came were looking for the gold; they did not (as do our contemporaries listed above) pretend to be alchemists.

THE PROBLEM WITH "TRAINING," OR "SLAVES OF THE ANT-GOD, THROOG"

Most of the exercises meant to teach one to act come through a devotion to the so-called Method.

Stanislavsky's pedantic teachings—that is, his trilogy—are, to a working member of the theatre, incomprehensible. His non-theoretical writings, on the other hand, such as *My Life in Art*, and those about him, *Stanislavsky Directs* by Gorchakov, et cetera, are quite illuminating.

Stanislavsky, like many of us philosophers, was barred by nature from pursuing his first love, action. Or, in his case, acting. Yes, we know he acted, but photos of him doing so display, to the knowledgeable, something other than a comet of the stage.

He took, as did many others, myself included, his love of the stage and his inability upon it, and turned that defect (a theoretical overview) that debarred him as a performer to good effect where it belonged, as a director. So far so good. He saw the play as a whole and tried to communicate his vision to the company.

Then, however, he tried to again abstract his ad hoc understandings (stand there, speak in such a way) and expand them into universal postulates. These are the musings of the theoretical about a process that is entirely physical and, let us say the word, almost entirely intuitive. Past telling the actor to fix his speech and posture, stand still, say the words, don't fidget, and have a general idea of the nature of the scene, there is nothing a teacher and little a director can do. The actor's teacher, past this, is the audience, which will administer its lessons, quickly, incontrovertibly, and bluntly; those so disposed will learn, and the others may seek work elsewhere.

The actor spends the nonperforming part of his day in rest, as he must. He may call this rest diversion, reading scripts, thinking about his part, or by any other name; but the true actor, in order to act freely and unreservedly upon the stage for two or four hours a day, must leave his mind clear and his body rested for the remainder.

Not so the director. So the mill of his mind, turning, turning, turning, may and usually does turn to theory and, so, to instruction. But there is, truly, little for him to instruct.

What is the play about, what is the scene about, stand there, move downstage of the couch on such a word, don't walk on the other fellow's laugh, the blue drapes rather than the red—that's about the limit of the director's actual job.

For the rest he is deluding himself. For like the plane in a spin, if the pilot gets himself out of the way, it will right itself.

The actor's true talent and job is to inhabit—whatever that may mean to him—the part. To stand still and say the words—in order to accomplish something like that purpose indicated by the author.

That's it.

A good rehearsal process will always end on a note of accomplishment, with the actors excited and not over-tired.

Thus they associate the scene, the line, the play, with accomplishment and are gently reminded, by the good director, of the truth; that truth being that they understand the play (they understood it when they *read* it), and that they need not strain themselves trying to bring some added intellectualization or "color" or "emotion" to the piece, that they themselves are suffi-cient, that they are actors.

The rehearsal of the scene, the line, the act, the play, must end with the actors happy and confident.

But most so-called training ends with the student disappointed.

I have never seen anyone actually *do* the Repeating Game. For the fortunate, this game calls for one student to comment on some aspect of the other student's appearance or demeanor—"You look rested"—and for the other student to repeat this phrase, "from his own point of view," until "something happens to make him change."

Now, I learned the rules from Sanford Meisner, who was my teacher, and who, I think, invented the game.

His object was to instill in the student the understanding that the words were not important, that the words were the responsibility of the author, and that all the actor need do was treat the words as if they were gibberish and react truly in the moment *to the other actor*.

A grand objective, and one shared by all directors, teachers, and theoreticians: how to help the actor, in Mr. Meisner's words, to "act truthfully under imaginary circumstances."

The problem lies in this: What is the meaning of "from one's own point of view"? What is the meaning of until "something happens to make him change"? Any and all students attempting the Repeating Game have their attention thrown back on themselves: "What *is* my point of view?" "Has something truly happened to make me change?" No one has ever done the Repeating Game successfully. Yet many of those who failed at the exercise can actually act. How? They are disposed to act, they love to act, they have studied voice, diction, dance, and analysis, and they have talent and will.

The game was the essence of the Neighborhood Playhouse understanding of the Method. That of the crosstown rivals the Actors Studio was "emotional memory."

Here, Lee Strasberg and his teachers and disciples strove for the same end—spontaneity under imaginary circumstances—by endeavoring to instill in the actor the ability to "remember" or "reexperience" a feeling something like what one might suppose to be felt by the character in the play. But all we know of the character is the lines he speaks.

The problem here is, What does "I love you" mean?

It may mean "Be mine"; it may mean "Leave me alone."

Further, a concern with one's own feelings makes one as boring on the stage as it does offstage. No one is enthralled by the specter of his fellow feeling something.

We go to the theatre to see action—we want to see what the characters *do*.

Here from Mr. Meisner and Mr. Strasberg we have two schools of understanding of the Stanislavsky system, Stalin and Trotsky, or Jung and Freud, if you will; but like communism, the idea, however presented, just does not work.

One cannot "become" spontaneous by studying self-consciously; one cannot fit oneself to perform the play by studying failure and trying harder. The teacher and, to the largest extent, the director are like the pilot of the plane who is convinced that a spin cannot be righted—but get out of the way and the plane will right itself.

To extend the conceit, the play is like the plane in this: If correctly designed, it will fly itself; and the consciousness of the actor, that is, one born to act, loving the play of it all, and happy to be on the stage playing, is a gift from God. It does not need the coddling and manipulation of those second-raters, the theoreticians, and I include myself, who are the conductor on the train but think themselves the engineer.

What is the best that we, directors and teachers, can do?

Simplify the process to allow the talented to thrive, hate like the plague any direction that makes the artist self-conscious, and end every teaching session and rehearsal on a note of happy accomplishment.

How can this best be brought about?

1. Never ask the actor or the student to do anything more complicated than opening a window.

2. Never let a false or self-conscious moment go by. Never "go on to the next thing." There *is* no next thing. The actor and the student should be helped to the understanding that every moment may and can occur naturally, easily, without taxing either the intellect or the soul.

EMOTION

Nobody cares what you feel.

Nobody cares what the doctor feels, nobody cares what the fireman feels, nobody cares what the soldier or the dentist feels. They are expected to do their jobs irrespective of what they feel, and, while doing their jobs, they are expected to keep their feelings to themselves. This circumspection is called self-respect.

And nobody cares what you, the actor, feel. You are expected to do your job, which is to show up and say the lines, playing the scene so that the audience can understand the play.

I believe that Stanislavsky may not have been a genius, but that he was both lucky and wise. He was lucky in the appearance of Anton Chekhov, whose plays sparked Stanislavsky's inspiration that acting need not be formalistic; and he was wise in his recognition, and in his restraint, in getting out of the actor's way.

How do I know he did so? Because the Chekhov

plays were successful. For most of us, performances of Chekhov's plays are lugubrious and dreadful. This is the result of actors and directors "ootzing" them, which is to say, adding their "good ideas" to plays that do not require them.

Was Stanislavsky a good director? Very probably, and I base my conjecture partly upon production photos of him as an actor. Judging from these photos he was most assuredly no good, putting him in the position of most of us directors (myself included) who, thwarted in their desire to play, were left with, finally, the desire to observe and admire.

I presume his actors were good because his theatre was famed and so he had his pick. Thus, like the Actors Studio and many other schools, credit would have redounded to a theory or ability of the organization that in fact was due (whether or not they were aware of it) merely to the talents and exertions of its artists.

The wise director is more like a coach than a choreographer. He selects for ability and works to induce the talented to unite toward a common goal: the play.

The amount of influence one can exert on an actor is minimal. He or she will bring to the role idiosyncrasy and ease, which are the biggest components of what we call talent. The coach may help the talented to excise bad habits (slouching, muttering, turning upstage, not finishing a line, moving without intention), but the talented actors must be dealt with gingerly.

To begin, they are the recipient of a gift, which must be respected and which is, in the largest measure, out of their control. A self-destructive self-consciousness can and will be induced in the actor by a theoretical or, indeed, long-winded discourse by the director.

What can the director do? Gently suggest the nature of the scene (a leave-taking, a dismissal, a plea, a reprimand) and block the damn thing, then go outside and smoke a cigarette. That's it.

Stanislavsky's theoretical books are a lot of trash. They are unimplementable and, thus, useless for the actor.

His great gift was his recognition of Chekhov. And it is Chekhov's plays that transformed acting.

THE MAP AND THE TERRITORY

Here is a teacher's awakening: It is enjoyable for me to formulate my ideas; it is useful for me to formulate my ideas; it is helpful to no one for me to formulate my ideas.

The two hardest parts of the writing of drama are (1) discarding all the notes and sketches, and writing "at rise" and (2) accepting the resulting draft and committing oneself to work on that, rather than bemoaning or exploring (which are the same) the difference between that draft and the (actually nonexistent) ideal foreseen version of the play.

This ideal play seemed real, but its existence was an illusion, much as one imagines the appearance of a radio personality. On meeting him one thinks, "That is not how I pictured you," but one did not picture him at all, one merely heard his voice. The idea that one pictured him does not emerge until one sees him in the flesh. The idea that one held a view on an actual yet-to-be-written play does not emerge until one sees the draft and thinks, "This is not it at all." (Had it actually existed, what would be the need of writing it?)

Acting training should (and actually might conceivably) teach the acolyte those few things that would allow him to overcome the gap between his feelings that the performance already existed and the actual requirements of the scene.

The scene requires his commitment. This commitment must, of necessity, be made while the actor is ignorant of what that commitment might entail. The difference between his preconceptions (actually, his reluctance) and the truth of the moment *is* the truth of the moment, which did not and could not exist before the moment and is made of those very things the unskilled and untalented would wish away. It is the quest for certainty that kills the scene.

The unskilled and untalented actor thinks that his devotion to preparation is of some worth. Past a rudimentary understanding of the thrust of the scene, it may actually be called cowardice.

How can the student actor know that?

He cannot.

Analysis may aid the actor only to understand the nature of the scene—not to play it. For example, the action in a scene may be characterized as *challenging* or as *beseeching*, each analysis may be borne out by the lines of the text and is a guide to the nature of the scene, but however the scene is named, it still has to be played.

(A romantic encounter might, again, be characterized as a *seduction* or a *courtship*; the pleasantries, the gestures, and the fetching of drinks or the holding out of chairs will have vastly different qualities in each.)

However the artist may understand the map, it is only a guide to his goal, to achieve which goal he is still going to have to go out in the mud and rain.

The map is not the territory.

The analysis is not the scene.

The actor might be aided by a teacher who exhorted him to pick up his cue, speak up, turn out, begin and end the line cleanly, and keep still. Beyond that there's not a lot that even the best acting teacher might do—for the interchange breaks down at the point of commitment, and while physical direction might be suggested, it will come to nothing if, when the bell sounds, the actor "just doesn't feel like it," or, in the excuse of the Method, "just doesn't feel his character would do that," or "just doesn't feel that he 'likes' his objective anymore."

We may note that the actor who "just doesn't like his objective anymore" is not unlike the newly married man who has fallen out of love with his wife. The two share this: Their new perception is fostered by fear—by the fear of that intimacy which has been brought to life by commitment.

Most presenting themselves as students of acting will never learn to act. That talent might be discovered or freed, or perhaps even shaped, but it cannot be inculcated. The greatest coach in the world cannot take a random sampling of hopefuls and teach them to throw the ninety-mile-per-hour fastball.

Those who have not been born to act—and many will discover other outlets for their devotion to the art—may (I instance myself) become directors or writers; for where, in the history of the world, do such come from except those ranks? There is no shame in that.

And the inspired, exploitative, or ignorant may and will continue to talk to students and put them through various exercises and call it "teaching acting," but I do not think it is.

THEATRICAL FORMS

The theatre exists to present a contest between good and evil. In both comedy and tragedy, good wins. In drama, it's a tie.*

Comedy and tragedy are both about fate. Both originated as part of religious ceremony, where fate was known as God. They deal with two different aspects of God, the first (Adonai), the god of love, and the second (Elohenu), the god of judgment.

Drama is about day-to-day life. Its motto, rather than "The gods will not be mocked," is "Isn't life like that?" Comedy and tragedy are concerned with morality, that is, our relations under God; drama with man in society. Well and good. However, drama, being the less tightly structured form, allows for infinite mitigation of even its social concerns.†

---

*In film noir, evil wins.
†Put slightly differently, the operations of God or of the Fates must resolve perfectly, like a mathematical equation—there can be no uncathected re-

45

Having cast off the strictures of a theocentric universe, the writer of drama is free to abstract from his work the concerns of even person-to-person (ethical) interactions, and stage, in effect, a refutation of the theatrical interchange (performance art), where, as in the wait for the descent of Moses from the mountain, the populace first built then swooned over its ability to worship an object of its own construction, the molten calf.

In drama run amok, "There is no God and we are all alone" (which is, essentially, a cri de coeur, or endorsement of God's power) becomes, "As there is no God, we may act as we wish" (which is a Marxist invitation to crime).

The danger of drama, then, as opposed to the stricter forms, is the enshrinement of the individual (dramatist, protagonist, and, indeed, audience) as all-powerful.

But the writer of the stricter forms must himself submit to the exigencies of the form. If he does not— that is, if he is not humbled before that greater than himself—how can he expect the audience to be?

The audience will not undergo anything that the

---

mainder. The movements of society may be appreciated, on the other hand, as a provocative but unresolvable observation.

protagonist does not undergo. For the journey is the same, and the audience members understand themselves to be the protagonist—as, indeed, for the length of the evening they are, for the drama is their dream, put forward by their representative, the dramatist; and we know that in our dreams each character stands for the dreamer.

The protagonist is, finally, nothing other than his journey, which is but an ordered dream of the writer, who has surrendered to and works to understand and clarify the structure of a moral interchange.

The theatrical interchange, then, is a communion between the audience and God, moderated through a play or liturgy constructed by the dramatist. The theatrical workers, actors, directors, designers, writers, then, are essentially the descendants of the priests and Levites of the ancient Temple whose job, like that of their forebears, the storytellers around the campfire, was to address the question, "What in the world is going on around here, anyway?"

Around the campfire as now, around the screen, this question may be addressed mechanically—"I see where this action always has that result" (the sheriff will eventually arrive and the maiden will be freed from the railroad tracks)—or spiritually—"There is a force at work in our lives whose operation I do not understand.

I see, however, that attempts to understand it bring order into what would otherwise be chaos, my terror at which, absent awe and submission, could be calmed only by a profession of my own omnipotence."

Drama, then, which at its best is a sad exploration of the fact that "life is just like that," may progress in degeneracy through wish fulfillment (the action film) and whining (the victim play), into nihilism (performance art and deconstructed texts)—son et lumière being but a way station on the road to the manipulated re-interjection of man-made (political) glorification of human will (the Nuremberg rallies).

The theatrical event is either consecrated to God (tragedy and comedy), with the cathartic potential of surrender, or to man, in which case it may be misused for any manufactured purpose from incitement to good works to incitement to murder.

For the empty or political pseudodrama does not start with a blank slate. As the audience, consciously or not, has come to the place where humans always come to hear the truth, the empty event begins with a rejection—the harangue taking place not at Hyde Park Corner, where one would expect it and analyze it with the conscious mind, but in the theatre, where, as in the church or synagogue, and for the same reasons, we have surrendered part of our rational capacity in return for the chance to hear a deeper truth.

The agnostic protests that the claims of religion are unprovable and impossible, and cites biblical recounting of miracles. Yet these are not the claims but rather the *poetry* of religion. A love letter is, factually, unprovable, but it is not meant to be a statement of physics, but of love. The unconvinced, who says, "I do not understand how your love can be as big as an ocean," is being not rational but objectionably obtuse.

The good news is that, while anyone can be the recipient, at any time or place, of unwonted, inconvenient protestations of love, no one comes into the theatre without a conscious or unconscious submission to the possibility of revelation (for if all the attendee wanted was the assurance of a bit of drama, he would have gone to a hockey game). But he came to the theatre. To participate in a celebration of mystery. And what are we to do about it?

TOTALITARIAN TENDENCIES

It is no accident that our current understanding of the interchange between the actor and the audience was born in a totalitarian regime.

Stanislavsky lived and flourished under the dictatorship, first of the tzar and then of the Bolsheviks.

His ability to stage works of actual content—that is, works addressing the underpinnings of human life: loss, desire, fear, greed, and their consequences—was limited by both the acts of the censor and by concern about the possibility of such acts.

It is no accident that the actual moral content of Chekhov's plays is rather moot. They survive as beautiful, masterful sketches about the human condition, but, empty of both theme and plot, they must have succeeded at the time of their birth, as they do now, largely through their ability to allow the audience the glimpse of ineffable human oddity and to understand it as a sort of truth. They are beautiful comedies, and the birth of the modern theatre, but they succeed partly as, far from being objectionable, there is nothing in them remotely quantifiable.

Under the Bolsheviks, the Moscow Art Theatre's ability to express anything about the human condition was completely curtailed; and we see in the growth of its studios and their directors, Meyerhold and Vakhtangov, that strain of modern art that veers toward the fascist (here called constructivism).

These directors, deprived by the state of any meaningful texts, staged circuses where the costume and the set became the prime players. In effect, they constructed mobiles and called them dramas.

We see their progeny today in performance art. But what *is* performance art? If it is dance, let it be called dance and set beside the work of Baryshnikov, Alvin Ailey, Merce Cunningham, and judged accordingly. If it is circus, let them sell caramel corn. Performance art is neither fish nor fowl, but the bastard child of Stalinist repression (plays with no meaning) and deconstructionism (plays with no text).

Deconstructionism, and existentialism, as far as I can determine, hold that there is no meaning in anything save that which the individual elects to bring to it.

This is, of course, intellectual and moral savagery, and grows from two somewhat connected sources. The first, as noted above, is the position of the artist under a totalitarian regime; the second is deconstructionism's utility for the second-class mind.

For though few can build a barn, anyone can set fire to it. And if this act is not brutal envy but an expression of Nietzschean freedom, that is, if the arsonist is not merely permitted his crime, not merely unpunished, but lauded, then many otherwise taxed by their unrealizable desire for status will start burning down barns (hence the situation of those studies once called the liberal arts).

Once there is no text (yet the two hours are still called "theatre"), once the text is mocked by vandals, once those vandals are honored as innovators, we are left not only with pageant, but also with pageant exploitable or understandable in service of some greater good (the Nuremberg rallies, the Million Man March, Woodstock, et cetera).

Here is the mainstream of totalitarianism: the notion that one submerges oneself in a group the purpose of which is action to an end either unquantifiable (change) or unsustainable (world peace).

Recall the feminists' "You just don't *get* it." What would have prevented them from a clear statement of their goals had those goals been realizable and laudable?

(Note, some of the goals *were*, and, being stated, were or are in the process of being realized: equal pay for equal work.)

Compare "You just don't get it," which is a mockery of a supposed antagonist for his lack of understanding of an inexplicable goal, with deconstruction, whose champions (including Derrida) said, "If you don't understand, then you *can't* understand."

But one *can* understand.

The theatre can be used to grasp power—*but only if it is allowed to function independent of the text.*

The productions of Stanislavsky and the studios, and the works of Eastern European constructivist and modernist directors, were allowed to pass the censor if the question "Does this contain a meaning harmful to the regime?" was answered (correctly), "No, it contains no meaning at all."

Well and good, if such shenanigans were limited to the time and place of communist oppression. However, the phenomenon of the nontext play migrated over here.

We find it in three strands. The first is the constructivist love of the large or tricky set. (On a university campus, speaking to a design class recently, I was asked what I thought of the theory that a stage set should exist as a work of art, independent of the play. I said I'd never heard it before, but it was a lot of hogwash. I was surprised to hear gasps.)

If the designer wants to function in that manner, there is an ancient and approved art form—it is called sculpture. For just as a play cannot be improved but only vitiated by the presence of sculpture on the stage, any actual sculptor would confirm that his work could be lessened only by staging a play around it.

No, the theatrical interchange exists to communicate the text (and so the meaning) of the play to the audience.

Anything that does not aid that interchange, detracts from it. The tricky set is an attempt to hijack the interchange. It is a survival of constructivism, of a time and a place when the text was suppressed, and its survival today is a form of deconstruction, which is to say vandalism.

The second strand of the totalitarian survival is the Stanislavsky Method.* We recall that Stanislavsky's interest in the psychology and inner life of the character occurred in a time of repression—when the salient fact of life, totalitarian rule, and, later, war and revolution, could not be addressed. Upon what, then, did

---

*I suggest that anyone interested in a further, somewhat more technical, discussion of the Method and the American actor look to my *True and False: Heresy and Common Sense for the Actor* (New York: Pantheon, 1997).

the director focus? He called it the inner life of the character.

But there *is* no inner life of the character, as there is no character. The character is only a few words of speech delineated on the page, that's all there is—and the Method's concern with the character differs not at all from the daydreams of a twelve-year-old girl, e.g., "I wonder what Rhett Butler would do if he lived now?"

We note that Rhett Butler never lived, does not live, and will not live, but that the illusion of a character was formed by the conjunction of the text and the performance of Clark Gable (who did not engage in a study of the character's inner life, but merely showed up and said his lines).

The persistence of an interest in the inner life of the character is a form of deconstructionism, which is to say a rejection of the text: For the good dramatic text is nothing but a succession of incidents (as per Aristotle) in each of which the hero is engaged in a clear and important goal. That's all there is. There is no character absent this, and to ratify the study of the nonexistent and unquantifiable (Who is to say where Rhett Butler might have gone to college? Or what sort of cologne he favored?) is to admit both fools and scoundrels into the theatre and invite them to hijack the text. The Method and its obsession with the imaginary also allow the theatre to devolve into solipsism. For the actor and director here are interested with neither the text nor the audience, but only with themselves.* They allow themselves, finally, to reject the demands of the stage, do what feels good, and call it technique.

The third strand of totalitarian propensity is the victim play. This play, at least, has a quantifiable meaning (such and such a group are oppressed, and well-meaning people must learn to overcome their prejudices and come to their aid), but it is a meaning that panders to the lowest in the audience (See how smart you are? You knew the deaf were people too . . .), calls it the highest (Aren't you proud of yourself? I, the author, am proud of you), and ejects the audience both feeling self-righteous and having ratified its potential for violence (How could that vicious school mistress not have seen that the deaf are people too? Why, I'd like to . . .). These issue plays, then, are a mild form of propaganda, not putting forth the views of the state but, perhaps more dangerously, positing the existence of and recruiting for that group greater than the state: the confraternity of the right thinking. This invitation is potentially the mild beginning of fascism.

*The audience members do not care, as they cannot see where Rhett went to college nor how the scene is somewhat like the actor's feelings for his aunt.

Totalitarian Tendencies

Should the theatre be political? Absolutely not. The job of the theatre is to investigate the human condition. The human condition is tragic: We are doomed by our own nature; and comic: We are doomed by our own nature, but grace does exist. The human is certainly not omniscient, neither as the individual, nor as the state, nor as those groups that would supersede the state; and our misperception of ourselves as gods superior to the text, or as demigods incapable of error and licensed to endorse the meaningless, enlists the theatre in service of totalitarianism.

REPRESSION

It is the immemorial dream of the talentless that a sufficient devotion to doctrine will produce art.

The anti-Stratfordian hobbies away his time collecting proofs that the fellow named Shakespeare did not write the Shakespearean plays.

This, like many a devotion to doctrine, is as attractive as it is endless; the happiness of the anti-Stratfordian comes not from any final, objective victory but from the honor of taking the field, as an equal, against an artist.

Like much of politics, this seems to be a bold declaration on the side of equality, but it is actually arrogance.

For the assault on Shakespeare could be mounted by anyone with sufficient leisure and insufficient respect, but only Shakespeare could have written the plays.

No, no, the detractors cry, he was uneducated and could know nothing of life (implied: as *I* do).

No, this intellectual will not be taken in by artistic accomplishment, for it cannot be quantified, and so must, to his superior mind, be viewed, until he passes upon it, as null and without worth.

The talentless, undisposed to accept an achievement they cannot understand, take refuge in political and religious theories. Political: The worth of the play is moot. What is important is the sex, gender, race of the playwright. (Pseudo)religious: The actual worth of the teacher (as demonstrable by the accomplishment of his students) is moot. All that counts is his orthodox devotion (to the Method, the Meisner technique, et cetera) or his place upon the apostolic succession: He is the student of the student of the student of X, who was a disciple of Lee Strasberg.

But on the stage, the very reference to one's heritage is an indication of wishful thinking. For the audience does not care to what school the players belonged, or what their principles are; nor does it care about the race, sex, gender of the playwright. It would just like to be entertained.

But those who have no gift as entertainers and yet will not go home, many of them pick up the shield and sword of the intellect.

•

The theater is, essentially, a deconstruction of the repressive mechanism, which is to say, of the intellect and its pretensions.

Freud reminded us that the repression is the neurosis and that, taking his cue from Rumpelstiltskin, if we name it, it may just go away.

This same mechanism operates in a setting not therapeutic but recreational, the theatre. Here we are presented with a problem—the dilemma of the protagonist—and our efforts to solve it may be seen as a simulacrum of the therapeutic process. The analysand comes to realize that his projections (feelings for or toward the analyst) are not caused by the analyst but are habitual distortions on his part (neuroses). In this recognition he, theoretically, becomes free of his belief in the analyst's power. And so, simultaneously, of that of his neurosis. The viewer of the play, even better, is freed at the outset of the interchange, for he is watching a play about someone else.

As he is not personally challenged, he is free to watch the interplay and wonder at the clear but fantastical interpretations the protagonists put upon life.

To bring about this state, to present this interplay clearly to audience members, to induce them to suspend reason and to watch the show, is difficult.

Those who can accomplish this trick are known as

artists; those who cannot may find for themselves another name, and, indeed, they do, presenting themselves as professors and critics and intellectuals.

These folks, neither creators nor audience, work to insert back into the dramatic interchange that very repressive mechanism it is the job of the play to cleanse.

All plays are about lies. A misimagined or misdescribed situation is presented to the hero, and he must either uncover the lie that engendered it (*Hamlet*) or strive to create those lies he thinks will extract him from the situation (*All My Sons*). When the lie is revealed, the play is over: The work of the repressive mechanism has been explored through play, and the audience has experienced both its power and its weakness, and has seen it defeated. So, though the play may not have dealt with his particular dilemma, the affected viewer leaves refreshed to find a vicarious victory over that species of torment he shares with the hero (consciousness).

The talentless want to reinstate the repressive mechanism itself, deconstructing the play to weaken the language, elaborating the set to distract from the text, explaining the play to the audience, and, in fine, working to rob it of its terrible assertion: that the mind, the morals, and the acts of man are imperfect and imperfectable, that we are incontrovertibly self-deluded, but that, nonetheless, grace can exist.

But neither grace nor revelation nor peace can come from the superior exercise of the very faculty of understanding that the play has been written to challenge.

A lack of talent is no crime, but neither should it be a license.

That those with no understanding of, love for, or true interest in the theatrical process preach and scold might be construed as proof of the theatre's power.

Shakespeare wrote that we are all "guilty creatures sitting at a play," at which play some nod in self-recognition, and some storm out of their seats, affronted and bent on revenge.

POLITICALLY CORRECT*

The essence of democracy is this: that the individual is free to embrace or reject, praise or abominate, any political position—that in this he is accountable to no one and need never, in fact, articulate his reasons or defend his choice.

That any political act could possibly be termed correct posits a universal, incontrovertible, superdemocratic authority—that is, a dictatorship.

Political correctness can exist only in (as it is the particular tool of) totalitarian oppression. The actual meaning of the phrase is "ideological orthodoxy."

Many of us have "good ideas," but those with a day job—in contradistinction to the ideologues—are impeded from inflicting them upon our fellow human beings.

*I am indebted to Paul Johnson, particularly the chapter on Brecht, in his *Intellectuals*, and to Thomas Sowell, for *Knowledge and Decisions*.

The theatre is a magnificent example of the workings of that particular bulwark of democracy, the free-market economy. It is the most democratic of arts, for if the play does not appeal in its immediate presentation to the imagination or understanding of a sufficient constituency, it is replaced. The theatre especially exemplifies the democratic free market in that interactions between playgoer and presenter, between consumer and purveyor, are immediate, unfettered, not subject to regulation—interactions do not require verification by third parties (the seller need not explain why he has presented his particular good, the buyer why he has chosen or rejected it).

There is an immediate feedback between parties to the transaction, and each will maneuver until he has achieved his particular end (for the audience, diversion, entertainment; for the artist, support) without recourse to logical, verifiable position statements. The interactions of the theatre, a free-market institution, resemble thus not a legal proceeding but a wrestling match.

In our free society, the theatre is free: to please, to displease, to affront, to bore, to succeed, or to fail according to no rules or pattern whatsoever. It is the province not of ideologues (whether in the pay of the state and called commissars, or tax subsidized through the university system and called intellectuals) but of show folk trying to make a living.

This is, in a democracy, as it should be. That a director is good at moving folks around the couch or a writer is skilled at snappy repartee does not qualify either to use the audience's time in preaching—indeed, a straight-up paying audience will (and should) not stand for such nonsense and will drive the pontificator into another line of work. Unless he is subsidized.

It is only in state-subsidized theatre (whether the subsidy is direct, in the form of grants, or indirect, as tax-deductible donations to universities or arts organizations) that the ideologue can hold sway, for he is then subject not to the immediate verdict of the audience but to the good wishes of the granting authority, whose good wishes he will, thus, devote his energies to obtaining.

See the spate of Soviet bloc directors and playwrights inundating our shores from the sixties on, staging, in effect, son et lumières onto which a captive audience was sufficiently bored into projecting meaning. See also their American imitators: mime troupes, puppet troupes, university-funded laboratories, agit-prop ensembles, et cetera, offering meaningless, essentially constructivist, spectacles, which the audience was invited (as under communism) to understand as ineffable presentations of the struggle against oppression—a struggle so deep as to be incapable of being expressed in mere words—a lot of jumping about.*

Since the fall of communism, these constructivist examples of text as oppression and text as inevitable purveyor of bias are supposed, by their current champions, to celebrate and raise consciousness to the oppression: not now of the workers by the capitalists, but of women by men, the East by the West, the dark by the light. The self-anointed champions of right thinking may function *only* in a state-controlled environment (or its simulacrum, political correctness), for an audience free to choose will laugh them to scorn.

Champions of so-called theory, whether feminist, Marxist, multiculturalist, or other, in an attempt (supposedly) to cleanse expression of bias, are involved in a postmodern rendition of book burning. For the question of art is neither "How does it serve the state?" (Stalinist) nor its wily modification into "How does it serve humanity?" but "How does it serve the audience?"

---

*Consider the more benign allied phenomenon of a director's setting the existing play in nontraditional form: *Hamlet* in space, *Othello* in a convent, any number of Chekhov plays in modern dress, et cetera, as if changing the costumes changed the play. These "good ideas" differ in extent, but not in intent, from those of the ideologues full stop: to usurp power from the text and impose upon the audience a view more advanced than that of the author.

Why?

No one, to date, has been able to figure out how to serve humanity. Those who have, most notably, gained power through their claims to do so are known as tyrants.

But one may strive to serve the audience and apply concrete tests to determine if one has succeeded. (Did they laugh, cry, tell their friends?)

Let us note that we laugh, sigh, cry, gasp as the unfolding of the play reveals to us the folly of our previously held views. This is the power of the dramatic presentation, whether the knock-knock joke or the Shakespearean tragedy: We are presented with a clearly defined statement of fact, e.g., there is nothing in the world that could lead me to doubt my wife's chastity. And we follow it, step by step, until it leads us to defeat and, so, to a recognition of the tragic (or comic) worthlessness of our reasoning process. At the end of this process (whether the joke or the play), we are relieved of the burden of repression this knowledge has exacted.*

---

*I was, latterly, teaching a class on dramatic structure at a Great University, and to my shame allowed the class to be hijacked by a young fellow who insisted that no teaching on the subject that did not insist upon the right of two homosexuals to kiss on stage could have meaning. Shocked by the kid's Jacobin vehemence, it did not occur to me to inform him that immemorial dramatic wisdom cautions against *anyone* kissing on stage. It's not interesting, and can only signal the conclusion of the play. The correct answer to him should have been, "Try it, watch the box office, and get back to me."

Consider, in opposition, pseudodramas, mixed media, performance art, agitprop, and other suggestions that there exists *a* politically correct view, and that the correct venue for such a view's airing is the dramatic arena.

These essentially meaningless spectacles, again, invite the audience (self-selected by the political views the members hold) to bask in a celebration of the death of meaning. They do not explore human interaction (the task of drama), which is to say, they do not investigate in order to arrive at a conclusion, but begin with a conclusion (capitalism, America, men, and so on, are bad) and award the audience for applauding its agreement.

The origins of today's political correctness may be found in plays and films of totalitarian regimes (notably of Stalinist Russia), which were created or endorsed by a state that needed to deny the possibility of unfettered human interaction—which needed to excise meaning from art.

Artists under these regimes, denied freedom of expression of their own ideas, were given the choice of thinking themselves fortunate in maintaining a state subvention and/or cunning in sneaking hypothetically antistate symbolism into the nice pabulum.

The ensuing pseudodramas were (and are) the epitome of the politically correct. They must be correct; as containing no meaning, they cannot possibly be proved wrong.

Drama is about lies. Drama is about repression. As that which is repressed is liberated—at the conclusion of the play—the power of repression is vanquished, and the hero (the audience's surrogate) is made more whole. Drama is about finding previously unsuspected meaning in chaos, about discovering the truth that had previously been obscured by lies, and about our persistence in accepting lies.

In great drama we recognize that freedom may lie beyond and is achieved through the painful questioning of what was before supposed unquestionable. In the great drama we follow a supposedly understood first principle to its astounding and unexpected conclusion: We are pleased to find ourselves able to revise our understanding.

There may be politically correct spectacle, but there can be no politically correct drama. The very term should occasion revulsion in anyone who values democracy and that most democratic of arts, the theatre.

GREAT AMERICAN PLAYS AND GREAT AMERICAN POETRY

As the British extended the Edwardian Era to last until the First World War, I will stretch twentieth-century dramatic literature these few years until the present. What are the great twentieth-century American plays, productions, and innovations?*

Here are my choices for Great American Plays: First, *Our Town*, then *The Front Page*, *Who's Afraid of Virginia Woolf?*, *A Streetcar Named Desire*, *All My Sons*, and *Doubt*. One might also mention *The Time of Your Life*, *The Boys in the Band*, *The Best Man*, and *The Women*.

What do these plays have in common? They are intensely American. That is, they both treat American issues and are written in an American idiom closer to real poetry than to prose.

---

*I will both assume that my work might merit mention and exempt it from consideration on various grounds.

The poetry of *Streetcar* (as that of *Death of a Salesman*) owes a rather heavy debt to the Romantic tradition; that of *The Front Page* and *Our Town* is as American as apple pie and stuffing the ballot box. It is the vulgate, and is as poetic as the sports page or the blues.

These plays also have a common devotion to dramatic form. The playwrights are telling a story through the structure of incidents, each of which is an attempt of the hero to advance himself closer to his goal.

Judged thusly, *Streetcar* is perhaps the weakest of the group. Q: Who is the Hero? What does he or she want? And what is he or she prepared to do to get it? A: We have three choices, of which Blanche must be the best. She wants a home. What does Stanley want? Peace? Sex? And what does Stella want? Stanley. The plot is something of a group effort, and moot, but Tennessee Williams, like Chekhov, falls on the excused side of the axiom "Any fool can write a symphony, but it takes a genius to write a tone poem." As per poetry, *Our Town* partakes of that somewhat American tradition of list or faux-artisan poetry, which was inflicted upon us by Walt Whitman and persists today in the pages of *The New Yorker* and other high-toned rags. It could be said to come out of Whitman via Edgar Lee Masters and reached its dramatic apogee in *Our Town* and, perhaps, *The Time of Your Life*.

Nothing wrong with it when done well (Saroyan) or magnificently (Williams), but I suggest that the true and great American poetry, onstage and on the page, is the vulgate, the actual language of the people, and that can be found only in the cultural anathemas known as popular entertainment.

This may be an appropriate spot for a diversion on that subject. The job of the dramatist is to get, and that of the actors and directors to keep, the asses in the seats. Period. That is what pays the rent. Whatever an individual may have to say, it will not be heard unless the audience is (a) there, and (b) paying attention. And no one pays attention to anything that bores them. Why should they? You won't, I won't.

The purpose of the theatre is not to instruct, to better, to expatiate. It is to entertain. The great artist in entertainment may receive and so transmit something of an unusual or deep understanding of human nature or even human destiny—that is, he may do something more than entertain. But this is not necessarily better than entertainment.

Joseph Campbell makes the point that perhaps comedy is a higher form than tragedy. For tragedy reminds us of the operations of the gods as judges; comedy, of their operations as forgiving parents.

No one born ever listened gladly to a boring lecture. And the truest and most indelible lessons we learn we teach ourselves—through shame and guilt (tragedy), and through the recognition of grace (comedy).

A play must not be a lecture, and anyone staging the thing in his garage will, self-schooled, learn this by checking the tin box at the close of the first weekend. (The school-bound, government-supported, or otherwise impaired are spared this lesson until the [unlikely] first contact with the actual world [the audience].)

Just as the subject matter must be other than a lesson, the dramatic poetry (the text) must be entertaining. It must move quickly (why linger on a point already made?) and possess all the fluidity, rhythmic forces, and tonal beauty of which the author is capable. This is to say, it would be good if the playwright could actually *write*.

Judged by these standards, it might be revealed that Eugene O'Neill's works are not the masterpieces some have held them to be (unless masterpiece is understood as museum piece, and culture as other than the way we like to do things around here).

What are our culture's masterpieces of poetry? They were written by Hank Williams, Muddy Waters, Johnny Mercer, Irving Berlin, Gus Kahn, Randy Newman, Carole King, Sam Cooke, and Leadbelly. These song lyrics are the highest poetry, and we remember them and sing them all our lives. They are the sound track of our lives and seem naturally occurring—as does any real art.

Today I passed you on the street
And my heart fell at your feet
I can't help it if I'm still in love with you

Let us leave T. S. Eliot, Ezra Pound, and all the other quitters who preferred Europe. *J. Alfred Prufrock* is no better or worse than a rap lyric. It *is* a rap lyric (try it). I say get wacky or get real. Wacky being Wallace Stevens and real Merle Haggard. *That* is the American way, and that is our real poetry, the poetry of the American people. What could be more entertaining? Nothing.

"I have always depended on the kindness of strangers" is a pretty good tagline (it is not the last line in the play, but it is the last line anyone remembers and so *should* be the last line in the play). But how can it compare with "The son of a bitch stole my watch"?

THE BATHING MACHINE

Early automobiles were called horseless carriages, and they sported, just behind the dashboard, a socket to receive a buggy whip.

Now, these early machines often broke down and had to be hitched to a horse, so the socket and the whip were by no means irrational. As the horseless carriages improved though, the socket endured past the time when a whip might have proved useful.

This was a technological survival—persisting until new technology rendered its continuation pointless.

The bathing machine was the survival of a cultural attitude. What was it? A small cabana on large wheels, designed to be pulled by draft horses into the sea, carrying one or more bathers. At the end of its journey the horses were turned back toward shore, and the rear doors of the cabana opened to allow the bathers to descend in some measure of privacy into the surf.

This was the conjunction of Victorian attitudes toward novelty and nudity.

Swimming (called, in Victorian England, bathing) was, for the bulk of the populace, new. The late-nineteenth-century railroads provided transport and the growth of the new middle class provided funds for a trip to the seashore. And prior to these, the folks did not "bathe."

Bathing was new and seemed to require the addition of at least some technology to shield the acolyte from the horror of the unbridled sea.

Additionally, the Victorians took (or only admitted to taking) their pleasures clothed. So to descend into the sea in a costume (however modest) covering less, or suggesting the presence, of the human form seemed other than the thing, and the bathing machine was a continuation of this nicety by other means.

As with the buggy whip and its socket, the passage of time rendered the bathing machine a relic, and a new generation, more accustomed both to swimming and to partial nudity, put the machine aside. (In the 1960s men stopped wearing hats. And looked back and said, "Why, again, did we wear hats . . . ?") In short, fashion changed.

But the passage of the (if not more repressive, certainly more culturally strict) Victorian age loosed emotions that must then and must still, for society to function healthily, be controlled and cathected elsewhere.

It was not that Victorians banished sex—indeed, the insistence on separation of sexes, strict examination of speech, the virtual upholstering of the female form ensured that sex was before the eye and on the mind each moment of the day—but that they controlled the endorsement of its polite expression or indulgence. In short, they had rules.

Now, those rules may have been obeyed, or not, but the presence of rules (which could be offended against only at the risk of shame, guilt, prosecution, or censure) ensured a uniformity of behavior that exempted the individual from constant and troubling self-examination. That is, the rules were clear and it only remained for people to elect whether or not to obey them.

The weakening of these rules (beginning at the end of the Victorian Era and burgeoning in the 1960s) left and leaves the individual rather constantly troubled on the subject of sex. (Consider the divorce rate, the teen pregnancy rate, the derogation of the male by the feminist, the decline in the marriage rate, the debate over gay marriage, abortion, et cetera.)

The human desire for sex is a constant. It did not change. But the rules were loosed, and havoc ensued, giving rise to the prevalence of counseling, relationship therapy, men's and women's groups, and a vast amount of blather.

THEATRE

The Victorian Era was a time, in Europe, of relative peace. Its end, and the attendant rejection of the doctrine of legitimacy and of empire, led to a century of war.

The end of the Victorian Era, as noted, also gave us Stanislavsky and Chekhov, who, coevally and simultaneously with Freud, rejected Victorian formalism and began to search for new inner and previously unsuspected explanations for human behavior.

New writers, actors, and directors, previously and throughout history concerned only with *form* (Where does one stand? When does one speak? What might one say?), became concerned, now quickly to the exclusion of all else, with motivation.*

We see this today, where enlightened stage folk, assured that they are there to investigate their characters, muck about for weeks trying not to rehearse the play but to invent or discover the correct way to conduct a rehearsal. (Think of the couple confused about the correct conduct on a date, as they are confused about its objective. As Tolstoy wrote in *War and Peace* that contemporary parents agreed that the old ways of choosing a mate were gone, and it would be ludicrous to engage

*See also the migration of this impulse to the courts, whose current concern with a perpetrator's childhood would have been incomprehensible to previous eras, who supposed guilt and punishment should be assigned upon determination of facts.

78

in them, one must operate according to the new ways—
but no one knew what these new ways were.)

So courting couples invent rituals (one of which is
the ritual abandonment of the courted woman after the
man has had sex with her). Similarly, the occupants of
the rehearsal room, searching for form, in the absence
of the practicable and in the presence of the frightening
(for are they not setting about the exploration of human
nature?), spontaneously invent that which, in its use-
lessness, may be compared to the bathing machine.*

The theatre, in transition from the known but discarded old to the unimaginable new—set free but
frightened—brings forth a new and comforting formal-
ity: Its bathing machine is an interest in "the character."

Remove from the schools, the texts, and from the
rehearsal room the mention of character (the bathing
machine), and the only change is that the occupation
becomes more enjoyable, the process of creation less
cumbersome, requiring less effort, less so-called preparation, and more immediate.

---

*Many, perhaps most, dreaming of a career in the arts will drop out not
because of the foreseen and much lauded drawbacks—criticism, uncertainty
of employment, rigors of the craft, fickleness of the audience, possible
absence of talent—but because they are unsuited for a life of self-direction.
The terrifying question to them is not "How may I serve my craft?" or even
"How can I make a living?" but "What am I supposed to do today?" A good
first step might be the reasoned elimination of the superfluous—one does
not need a horse to go swimming.

THEATRE

Most directors and teachers make their living describing or refining the bathing machine. The wiser individual will see it for the anachronism it is and merely throw it out.*

A person speaking French does not say to himself, in the midst of conversation, "What is the third-person masculine plural of *to be*?"

And referring those interactions in a play that we would have progress toward spontaneity to the conscious, analytical mind is, similarly, a supererogatory act of folly. It is the bathing machine.

The water, however, is still there, and one may go right in. One does not require equipment but the insight and bravery to perceive that one does not require equipment.

---

*A concern with the character may describe attributes of a fictional being, which attributes the (good) dramatist has been at great pains to expunge from his text, as he knows that the audience does not care. All it cares about is what happens next. The better the dramatist, the less the narration.

So a concern with character might be likened to that interchange found in the works of those great Victorians, *Monty Python's Flying Circus*.

In *Life of Brian*, a bunch of Christians are being marshaled for execution. A centurion stands in front of two doors, one marked CRUCIFIXION and the other marked FREEDOM. The condemned come through, and each is asked "crucifixion" or "freedom"? Each replies "crucifixion," but one responds "freedom." The centurion remarks, "Oh, well, that's jolly good. Well, off you go, then." The convict says, "I'm only pulling your leg. It's crucifixion, really," and goes to his death.

STAGECRAFT

Every working organization differs in the way things are described in the front office and the way they actually occur on the assembly line. The newly minted private or second lieutenant, if wise, will stand back, shut up, and pay attention to the old sarge.

The Jewish tradition defined the apprentice interaction thus: Find a rabbi, do as you're told, and don't ask questions. This last, to me, is the only possible improvement on the Socratic system: for here the student not only answers his own questions but also asks them.

Stagecraft can be learned only onstage, in front of (as before) a paying audience. For as in most things it is the blunt trauma of failure that is the necessary spur to knowledge.

Why, the actor asks, does this laugh not work? Why do I feel the audience's attention lag at such point? Why does another actor get the notices, which I lack?

The answer may be a faulty understanding of the play, misblocking,* or, indeed, lack of acting ability.

And the cure may be stagecraft. This is neither acting nor analysis but simple, mechanical technique. How does this differ from acting?

Thusly: The surgeon studies anatomy and surgery in school, in the lab, and in the dissecting room. He learns many things there but might *not* learn to double-check the number of prepared sutures before cutting, or to open the patient *briskly* in order to have more time available for work on the critical aspects of the procedure.

The boxer may train forever in the gym, but it might take an actual apprenticeship in competition to teach him to end the round at his own corner, so that the other fellow has to take a walk to get a rest.

These perhaps do not rise to the grand level of technique, but they are of a status greater than tricks and are always practicable and will improve any performance and its reception.

Always gesture with your upstage hand. This opens one out to the audience.

Never stand either parallel or perpendicular to the

---

*Misblocking or misdirection must be dealt with by the actor, who is going to meet a lot of bad directors in his time. And he is going to have to learn how to deal with these, as he is going to have to learn to deal with bad, thoughtless, or inefficient actors, producers, managers—in short, with life.

downstage lip. As in boxing and dance, this renders the body dead and flat-footed.

Stand at an angle. Diagonals are powerful.

Take the scene off with you. Your scene ends not when you have finished speaking or when you "leave the room," but when you are out of sight of the audience.

Keep your eyes up. The audience does not want to gaze at your forehead. The eyes, being the mirror of the soul, are what the audience came to see.

Don't gesture. Many actors wail around onstage like cuttlefish on uppers.

Relax, keep your arms and hands still; then if you make a gesture sometime in the play, perhaps the audience might pay attention.

PICK UP YOUR CUES

It is virtually impossible (given good diction) to speak too quickly on the stage. Most actors pause before each line. Why? Pick up the pace. Nobody pays to "see you think."

Speak up. Electronic amplification has done more to ruin the American stage than all the Soviet bloc directors combined. The playwright wrote the lines to be said out loud.

Here is the corollary: Hit the final consonant. Most

actors, lacking good diction, swallow their final consonants and the last one or two words in the sentence.

Many may think this is being natural. But there is
nothing in the world natural about being onstage.
You're there to put on a play. Speak up, and speak out.
Hitting the final consonants teaches one of the most
important lessons in music: End the phrase. And the
corollary, start the phrase: When it's time to speak,
speak out. Commit yourself to the phrase, and you
commit to the play. That's all there is.

Never walk on a laugh (yours or, God forbid,
another's). Many actors try to fill what they consider an
awkward pause (a laugh) by taking stage. And one can
do this by a movement as slight as a turn of the head.

The audience at the comedy came to laugh. *Let* it.
Movement of any kind—a slight readjustment of posture, for example—kills the laugh dead. You are not
being asked to freeze but to relax. Never walk on a
laugh.

And never walk on another actor's lines. The playwright wrote the lines for the benefit of an audience. If
you are moving, the attention will go to your movement
and away from the line. (You may be directed to break
this and some or all of these other infallible rules by
some director, at which point you will be taxed to learn
not only stagecraft but also philosophy.

Stagecraft

NEVER APOLOGIZE DURING A CURTAIN CALL

The curtain call is not an applause meter but a recognition of the audience. You are there to thank the audience for its attention.

Many beginning and bad actors use the curtain call to communicate to the audience that they are sorry about their performance and know they should have done better. Stand up straight, don't fidget, and bow your thanks to the audience for its attention. Further, when you go off, keep your head up and exit with dignity. The audience's enjoyment of a perfectly good play (and of a perfectly good performance) can and will be lessened by your indication (through slouching, head hanging, or pushing the other actor to hurry and get off so you can hide yourself) that "I guess it could have been better."

If it could have been better, make it better next time. Your whimpering to the audience can do nothing but decrease its enjoyment of what may, in fact, have been a perfectly good performance on your part, and an enjoyable evening on its.

The worst-case symptom of this apology is picking something up. Many amateur and not a few unschooled professional actors will, on leaving the stage after a curtain call, pick up a prop or piece of costume. Oh,

85

please. This is not your job; it's the job of stage management. It means only: I'd like to do more.

Well, you had your chance, and you will have another chance at the next performance. (We see this miching behavior also in actors who, at the audition, can't get out of the room.)

Many beginning actors, and many of the aged, will finish their audition, leave the room, and come back for their forgotten scarf, script, fox terrier. Don't do it. If you were dumb enough to leave it there, forget it, forfeit it, and so teach yourself never to do it again.

DON'T LAUGH. DON'T CRY.

Nobody comes to the theatre to see actors laugh or cry. They come to laugh or cry themselves.

The most ancient and correct theatrical aphorism is, "If you laugh, they won't. If you cry, they won't." And it's true as sunrise. Beginning students tax themselves with "learning" to cry, and "What do I do if they ask me to cry?"

Figure it out. But if, in effect, "ordered" to cry by the director, I suggest you treat it as a physical rather than emotional request. That is, if the character must sneeze, you could do without a complete psychoneurotic self-dialogue about whether or not you "feel" like it. What is to prevent you from treating a direction to cry (or laugh) similarly?

Don't, for God's sake, fidget. Nobody cares about your precious aperçu about the way the character might have played with the toggle on her duffel coat. Who gets your attention at the party? The boy or girl who is doing interesting things? Or the one with sufficient self-respect to sit quietly?

ALWAYS TAKE YOUR WALLET ONSTAGE

George Burns said this was the most important thing he had learned in eighty years in show business.

There are, I am sure, many more examples of stagecraft that will occur to me when I have finished this book, but they and their like will all be learned by the honest devotee of the art, serving apprenticeship on the professional stage. Good luck.

IMPERTINENCE

That a director would do something "interesting" with a script is worse than heresy—it is impertinence.

For, as Stanislavsky said, "Don't touch it unless you love it." The exploding set, the play set in space or in the future, all these refuges and cloaks of the untalented, all of these dodges fail the test. The test is: Do you love it? Would you, the director, designer, producer, bet your soul on it?

The rabbis said: You have been told that only the high priest could enter into the holy of holies on the Day of Atonement. No one else would or could risk entering, for anyone blemished by the slightest sin would, upon entrance, be struck dead by God.

We know, the rabbis said, that you don't believe it, but this is the question: If the Temple still existed, would you chance it? Would you risk your life and soul merely to prove your assertion that God did not exist?

The question, to the hack, is ludicrous, but the artist knows the answer.

Impertinence

The Temple has always been full of the moneylenders. Every generation starts fresh and begins by simultaneous acts of creation and rejection.

The student-intellectual, protected by those he is, finally, paying to coddle him, can indulge in all sorts of both pointless and destructive whimsy and conjecture. The true devotee of the art, he who has run away from home, will learn, if he wishes to stay, to keep his mouth shut, his eyes open, and to obey his superiors. If he wishes to stay he may of course be exposed to bad examples, but the leisure afforded by his silence and subservience may be employed in a contemplation from which the exercise of his voice might debar him.

THE END OF ADOLESCENCE

The ancient parental adage is that the children are never listening, but they are always watching.

Animals learn from observation: what to fear, what to chase, how and to whom to display deference or aggression.

The last natural period of matriculation between the adolescent and the adult state is seventeen to twenty-two years old—the period of attendance at college.

The lessons imbibed (here I differentiate between knowledge gained in classrooms, if such there be, and knowledge assimilated without thought from observation of the relationship among peers and between the young and their elders) are virtually indelible.*

---

*Consider this: We hear a joke that begins, "Two guys go to a thrift store, and one of them says . . ." Years later we hear the same joke, beginning, "Two guys go into a clothing store," and suppress (or, indeed, fail to suppress) the impulse to correct the joke teller for his inaccuracy.

The End of Adolescence

If we imbibe, in college or through training at that age, a belief in the perfectibility of art and the artist, we will be hard-pressed in later life to adopt a more practicable view.

Art is about the spontaneous connection of the artist to his own unconscious—about insight beyond reason. If his insight were reasonable, anyone could do it, but anyone cannot. Only few can, and they are called "artists."

The only purpose of technique is to allow the artist to bypass the conscious mind. Vocal technique allows the actor to cease wondering if he can be heard or understood. Physical technique allows him faith in his own ability to move and stand simply, gracefully, and relaxedly.* The purpose of yoga and its myriad poses and adjustments, we are told, is to allow the yogi to focus on his breath.

Drama is a mystery. It is an exploration (undertaken by both the artists and the audience) of the unconscious. Outside of the work done on simple, physical adjustments (voice and diction and speech),

---

*A friend in the Special Forces explained to me that the Olympian conditioning they undergo is, in the main, to allow a freedom of thought, so that upon seeing an obstacle, the conscious and unconscious mind are free to think, "How best can it be overcome?" rather than, "There is no way in the world I could surmount that."

the work of the play should be done by the writer—
freeing the actor to play. There is, in truth, no "emotional" work or "preparation" done by any actor that can
be better than his spontaneity, just as it requires a very
good set indeed to be a better platform for presentation
than a bare stage, and a great direction to be better
than silence.*

The Bible admonishes us that when we are faced
with temptation, to flee from it.

What happened in Chicago? In the late sixties and seventies a bunch of young people started putting on plays.
We came of age in a time of abundance, menial jobs
were plentiful, and we all worked day jobs and pooled
our income and put on plays. We encouraged one
another, worked in one another's theatres, and were
inspired to write, direct, produce, and design one another's shows.

There was no money to be had in the presentation
of plays (our most fantastical aspiration was to have a
month where receipts paid the cost of production), and
there was no fame past the regard of the (generally

---

*Most so-called direction is a reiteration of the text. It reads, "I love you,"
and the director says, "You see, here he is expressing his feelings." As if the
actor could not read.

neighborhood) audience. There was time (we were having the time of our lives, what else was there to do?), and space (rents were low, there were transitional areas, not quite slums, but not yet gentrified) was cheap.

In *Outliers*, Malcolm Gladwell writes of the conditions necessary for expertise. One is ten thousand hours of practice (the Beatles playing thousands of hours on end in Hamburg; the young Bill Gates stealing time on his high school computer). And that is what we had in Chicago, years of putting on plays continually. So we learned not only the crafts of the stage (speak up, stand up, stand still, turn out, and pick or write a play interesting enough to hold the audience's interest) but also the lessons of theatrical administration: how to advertise, what to charge, how to maintain a space, what to present, how to plan. We had to, as there was no one there but us—an inestimable experience and a true education, for when one's livelihood depends upon it, one does not have to be shown something twice. (The college student or otherwise subsidized individual playing at theatre may defend—to himself, his teachers, or his audience—the text or staging of a play whose theoretical worth may theoretically be great but whose ability to entertain is negligible. In the actual theatre, if they didn't come, you're done. Figure out why and either try again or go back to law school.)

Joe Mantegna, Meshach Taylor, William Petersen, William H. Macy, John and Annie Cusack, Lonnie Smith, Laurie Metcalf, Dennis Franz, Dennis Farina, John Malkovich, Linda Kimbrough, Mike Nussbaum, Gary Sinese, and I were all part of the phenomenon of Chicago theatre. We brought little intellectualization (prejudice) to it and so were fairly unencumbered when it came to an examination of the facts: The community had said, "Interest me, and I'll come," and so we strove to do so.

We had youth, strength, and exuberance, and we had not been ruined by bad training, which is to say, by a search for the perfect moment, beat, line, performance. We'd been privileged to have done what every member of show business has done since the beginning of time: We'd run away to the circus—and we were staying. What fun.

SUBVENTION

A subscription audience is a dreadful audience. It is almost inevitably sullen. Why? It has been dragged out of the house. These subscribers are not theatergoers, though they may again be, under different circumstances; they are bargain hunters, who've been sold a bargain. "Six plays for the price of five" sounds like a good idea at the time, but in practice it functions like "all you can eat," where the only way one can make sure one has gotten one's money's worth is to make oneself sick. All you can eat is a come-on, and, as the restaurant-goer eats on, he recognizes it as such, and each mouthful, as he nears repletion, reminds him that he has been conned.

Six plays for the price of five rewards the canny bargain hunter when he sends his check, and punishes him as the time to present himself in the theatrical precincts comes near. For he, of old, left the house to go to the theatre only with a sense of excitement—to see that which was new, and touted (by the press or, better, by his friends) as unmissable. This urge to adventure was and is a delightful part of the theatrical experience. It is romance, and it presents itself to the theatergoer in the audience exactly as it presents itself to the happily courted at a first date: Here I am—delight me. But not to the subscription ticket holder. No. He had made his plans sometime in advance; there was no romance to begin with, just the low-level acceptance of a moderate bargain. Worse, the time has now come, and he is not in the mood. How do I know? Because "the mood" is confected of novelty, the desire for the scarce, and the urge to adventure. The decision to attend was made long ago; there is, therefore, no adventure. And how scarce can something be that must be hawked as "fifteen percent FREE"? No, the subscription holder has been conned and knows it. He would much rather stay home and exercise his God-given right to decide how to spend his evening. He's sold that right for a mess of pottage. He shows up sullen and *stays* sullen. He will not relax; the magical intercession of the ticket price happened long ago and, if remembered, is regretted. He will sit judgmental during the performance, applaud only grudgingly, and bear his grudge all the way home and through the remainder of the evening— this grudge is now the only thing he will enjoy, and what's more, he has paid for the privilege. No. No. No.

Subvention

Subscription audience = bad audience. This is the beloved child of the administrators, and, to them, subscriptions make undeniable sense. How much better, they reason, to get the money up front and in the bank, and to avoid the risk that one unacceptable play might sink the theatrical enterprise. But such is the nature of the theatrical enterprise: If the audience doesn't come, the play must be taken off; for how might it support a theatre to have the management insist that an unacceptable performance continue? The only audience that will persist in patronizing such a theatre has been dulled, suborned, and has forgotten the essence of the interchange, which is the possibility of being delighted. Such come to the theatre not to be delighted, but—in the lay communities—as they go to the dentist, because it is "good for them," and, in the university communities, to display professional resistance to the plebian lure of mere enjoyment, and their stalwart, Stakhanovite support of "culture."

The subscription series is the devil's bargain. For those employed it pays the rent, but as it protects them from the risk, it deprives them of the thrill of an actual, excited, live audience.

Government subsidy functions similarly. Money is all well and good; the desire to become self-supporting is a

good goad toward theatrical success, its necessity an
inestimable goad. So why not take the money from the
government? I did. I got a grant, as a beginning writer,
from the New York Council on the Arts. The grant was
$4,000, which was around eight times more money
than I had ever seen in my life. It supported me for
quite a while, and I was, and am, somewhat grateful to
the State of New York, and perpetually indebted to the
arts administrator who bent every rule to put the
money in my pocket. And my plays have been produced
at theatres accepting both government grants and possessing subscription audiences. But, whore that I am, I,
having taken and spent the money, will report what I've
seen.

Grants accrue, logically, to arts organizations that
have a history of artistic success (subjective) and of
longevity (objective). The grants, then, do not and *cannot* generally come in the moments of truest need—the
initial periods of the individual's or organization's pro-
ductive life. They seem to come, if they come, just
around the time the organism no longer needs them—
that is, at the time it first becomes viable—that is, "too
late." Well, better late than never, you say, which is true
and addresses the objective criterion. But what about
the other one? Who *gets* the grants? They are awarded
by committees, the committee members chosen by

committees. There must, then, be consensus, which is
to say compromise, choices. (How could it be otherwise? It could not.) But would the arts organization
plumping for grants not then form and/or present itself
in a way calculated to garner the approval of the particular committee? To do otherwise would be folly; and to
do so the arts organization itself must—to differing
extents but positively—reconstitute itself as a grant-
writing committee. What was it previously? Previously
(poor, ill formed, newborn, struggling), it was a group
led by a hegemon. Who was this individual? He was the
force (writer, director, actor, designer) whose vision
compelled and directed the energies of the group. This
person, in the days of yore, was known as the director,
as he *was* the director. And he held sway because and
as long as his vision—expressed in practicable terms—
seemed exciting and right to the group.

These practicable terms were, "Do this play, do it
such, stand there, paint that wall red, say the line thus,"
et cetera. His vision—usually inchoate but on some
level understood—was found beautiful by the group
and, in presentation, was found beautiful by the audience. And so the new theatre prospered. As it did, it
attracted first neophytes, and then sycophants, and
finally support personnel.

These support personnel were first called production assistants, gofers, helpers; later, production staff; and ultimately, as it says in the Bible, "The time will come when you will wish to elect yourself a king." This production staff, as the theatre grew, looked for support and direction not to the *artists*, but to their *own* kind and elected a new king, and this king was called the managing director.

Where previously tradition, use, and common sense dictated that a theatre could have but one head, now it had two. And the new coequal title managing director rendered nugatory the title director. For it was clear what the managing director did: He managed. But that was the old-style, unadorned director's job. And so his title was changed to artistic director and the child had two mommies. Now, instead of a coherent whole, we have a committee. The committee, to compound the enormity, has two heads, and as we know from experience, a committee with two heads has (declared or not) one head, and that will be the head who is better qualified to function in a committee.

The artistic director (ex-director) had or has a vision, but that vision is inchoate: Why do this play rather than that? Why paint the wall red rather than yellow? He cannot say, and so he will be shouted down in committee. But the decisions, ruminations, and directions of the managing director are quantifiable: A subscription audience will ensure income, as will a government grant, as will an intelligent pitching of the plays' or season's content to a wider group (for why alienate any potential audience?). This managing director and his constituency are the only portion of the organization suited to promote the organization. Not only will they succeed in committee, the choices they make for the distribution and use of the funds their efforts have brought in must tend toward the organizational.

Note again: The money, to their minds, came in not because of the excellence of the productions but because of the efforts of the administrative staff. The obvious use of the incoming funds, thus, is to increase the administrative staff.

At this point in the entertainment we see the birth and growth of various programs: young audiences, diversity, outreach, a theatre school, and so on.

What of the artistic director (ex-director)? Well, he'll most likely either quit ("What happened to my theatre?") or be replaced by action of the administrator in concert with the board, which he has brought into being—such board composed, of necessity, of businesspeople making business decisions. For while the task of the artist is to create, the task of an institution is to continue.

THEATRE

The perfect theatre, the Great Theatre, will sprout forth spontaneously from the unquenchable desire of one or a few to bring their visions to the stage. If successful, it must attract those forces that will, eventually, lead to its destruction. But, then, like all other organic life, it was never designed to live forever.

TWO TEACHERS

I tried teaching writing twice. Once was at Yale, in the seventies, in the Graduate School of Drama; the second time was in the writers room of a television show. I failed both times. And I wondered why.

The rules of dramaturgy, as I understand them, could not be more clear, and anyone who wanted to learn, I thought, would clutch them to the chest, weeping in thanks, and scurry off to the pen and paper. But no. The rules, I realized, through much trial, were not the problem. The problem, of course, was the teacher.

Jujitsu is a beautiful art. It cannot be learned from a book but must be demonstrated by a teacher. It can be learned only through the repeated attempts to apply the techniques shown upon an opponent who would much rather you did not.

Medicine, similarly, may be studied in lectures and books, but may be learned only through attempts to apply the technical to actual living, complicated human beings, who are worried and confused, and whose life and happiness are in the balance.

Who are the correct teachers of writing? There are two.

It's written in the Koran: The Prophet leaves two teachers, a speaking teacher and a silent one. The speaking teacher is the Koran, and the silent one is death.

Similarly, the dramatist has two teachers: The speaking one is the audience.

The best laid plans go merrily agley. And all the assurance, talent, and labor in the world may and will be overridden by the audience.

This is not to say that the audience will say of a beloved piece of work, "I hate it," which may happen irrespective of (and indeed in tribute to) the artistic success of the piece, but that the moment, gag, turn, transition, act ending, surprise, et cetera, however theoretically well crafted, may not actually work.

Of these the audience (before it leaves the theatre and puts on—as do you or I—its wise, critical hat) is the only judge. If the audience members didn't laugh, it wasn't funny. If they didn't gasp, it wasn't surprising. If they did not sit forward in their seats, it wasn't suspenseful.

Two Teachers

The audience will teach the writer, as its judgment, moment by moment, is the only test. If the audience goes to sleep, the play is done, no matter that it "picks up" in the next scene.

In this the dramatist is like the surgeon, whose technique, however admirable in the abstract, must be judged primarily by whether the patient lived or died.

This is the dilemma of the theatre school. Music and dance may exist independent of the audience, the feedback of which, while important, is not essential to the performance. But the actors onstage, in front of a paying audience, pace themselves, restage themselves, and reinvent the performance constantly in response to an actual, living organism: the audience at that particular performance.

The audience, in the actual theatrical interchange, must have two qualifications: (1) it must have come to be delighted, and (2) it must have paid for admittance.

If the audience is suborned (that is, under the sway of any direction other than its will to be pleased), it cannot participate in the interaction. The audience surrenders its rationality, just as does the child hearing a bedtime story, in response to the promise of enjoyment. The teacher, critic, competition judge, assembly of fellow students all watch the performance in order to judge, and so their opinion, either of the moment or of the piece as a whole, is worthless.

THEATRE

The audience must have paid.

Why? In order to allow magical forces to work.

The magician waves his magic wand, and the coin vanishes. If he did not wave his wand, the audience might correctly assume the coin must be in the other hand (as, indeed, it is). But the wand suggests the operation of some intervening force sufficiently powerful to suspend the operations of the world as we have come to know them. The phrase "once upon a time" operates in exactly the same fashion—as, to a lesser extent but nonetheless, does the phrase "my fellow Americans."

The magical phrases are an inducement allowing the audience to self-suggest the operations of another world.

The ticket price is a sacrifice entitling the audience to that enjoyment.

The audience members must pay. The payment transforms them from critics to entitled consumers. In the car business they teach that "nobody walks on the lot unless he wants to buy a car." The equivalent of walking on the lot is payment for admission.

The audience members coming to be delighted, and paying for the privilege, will eke from the drama the enjoyment to which they are entitled. If the drama is not enjoyable per se, they will read the program, go to sleep, or leave.

So the wise dramatist will *watch* them and learn from their spontaneous, visceral reactions: Is the scene too long, unclear, ambiguous? Is the punch line one beat too soon or too late, one syllable too long? Does the audience anticipate him, does it care? Now, just as the audience must pay, the playwright also must pay, for "experience is the name everyone gives to his mistakes."

What does the playwright pay? He ventures his good self-opinion. He bets his self-regard upon the success of the play and its various twists, turns, structure, rhythm, and gags. And when he fails, when the audience withholds not its approval, which is bad enough, but its attention, the playwright suffers hot shame and vows never *never* to subject himself to this again. That is the lesson of the speaking teacher.

The silent teacher is the empty page.

A CULTURE OF CONFESSION

What is guilt, if not a desire for punishment?
                                                —Ruth Wisse

Most of that which passes for acting training is an exercise in confession. In the so-called Method, the student is instructed to find incidents in his life like those the character is undergoing in the script. The student is then urged to explore these real-life emotions in the presence of teacher-director, in order to become closer to the character. (1) Fine and good. But there is no character. There are only words on a page. And (2) Who wants to go to the theatre to see people crying?

What is the provenance of this desire for so-called emotional truth? It is psychoanalysis. In the theatre or studio the "Method"-director-teacher stands in for the psychoanalyst and invites the subject to confess. The supposed aim of confession in psychoanalysis as in

Method acting is freedom from inhibitions and, thus, an increased ability to attend, happily, to the business at hand (life or the play).

But neither psychoanalysis nor the Method actually works. They are both interesting models for the understanding of human behavior, but neither functions well in practice. For the question in each is, "Now what?" The analysand discovering at long last that the cause of his unhappiness was his overbearing mother; the method actor finds that the mad scene of Ophelia is not unlike the time her kitten died. They still have to get on with it—life or the play. The question, for both, is "Now what?"

Both psychoanalysis and the Method free the subject from the need for action. The actor, in a state of nature, will study to perform the play, and any analysis or cogitation not to that end will be understood, correctly, as waste. But the Method actor is excused from that sense of urgency which a desire for an actual performance career might entail, and is offered in its stead: guilt. This guilt expresses itself as not having done enough or not having understood or undergone the emotional experience sufficiently deeply—it is felt as a sense of "always having more to do."

Well, the answer here, plainly, is more study and more dedication to the idea of an emotional understanding, i.e., more training, and more rehearsal. Note that in the actual production, at some point the actors and director stop farting around and actually rehearse the play. Which is to say, they decide where they are going to stand and when they are going to move (the remainder of the theatrical magic being accomplished by the text laboring heroically against the actors' good ideas.)

The analysand mouldering in the psychoanalyst's office is excused from answering the question: What do I actually want, and what am I prepared to do to get it? As is the addicted Method actor. The freeing question is: What does the character want, and what am I (his simulacrum) prepared to do to get it? This gets one off the couch and out of the rehearsal room, while the guilty takes on himself the woes of the world and, in so doing, both excuses and aggrandizes himself, and his inactivism.

We note the same in much contemporary liberal thought: Everything is always bad, and that the wise liberal is aware of it and so somehow more worthy than those who are not.

This worthy person actually does nothing to alleviate the woes he professes to perceive (global warming, hunger, poverty, social injustice), finding the mere profession a more than sufficient proof of worth. This is the meaning of candlelight vigils, "walks for," and Live Aid concerts, which, like charity banquets down through history, are merely a celebration of the excellence of the hosts.

The commoditization of guilt in psychoanalysis and the Method are coeval, beginning with Freud and Stanislavsky in late nineteenth-century Austria and Russia. Each recognized that the human being makes decisions based on an inner (unconscious) picture of the world, and that by observing the individual's otherwise incomprehensible actions, one may determine the assumptions upon which these actions are based. Well and good, but psychoanalysis's clientele, then and now, in the main, is the overindulged, sated, self-involved individual who simply substituted, for a few hours a week, the self-indulgence of the couch for that of the wider world. This consumer recognized that an amelioration of his state would bring about the abandonment of those happy several hours a week devoted to the ultimate in self-involvement.

But, as it would be inconvenient for him to admit that the time on the couch was entertainment, he called it trauma and held himself to blame for an inability to be completely forthcoming. He discovered the pleasure of guilt. As does the Method actor, who not only can always do more, but will not move (act) until he sees his way absolutely clear (usually never).

Another strand in the discovery of the inner life was

communism. Coming of age, like its yoke mates, in the early twentieth century, communism exploited, as a tool of impressment and control, the confession.

Individuals professing allegiance to the tenets of Marxism-Leninism were regularly forced to confess their various sins of action and thought to the group. Those who were insufficiently forthcoming or were reluctant (who wanted, in effect, to retain their psychic integrity) were shamed or shunned, or "corrected," until either they accepted (or pretended to accept) the group verdict, left, or were expelled from the group, or were shot.

For, here, to go deeper meant to experience guilt. And, as with acting and psychoanalysis, the guilt need not come from actual wicked actions; it could come from the very inability to "go deeper."

But if your mother did not sufficiently love you or if Ophelia's abandonment by Hamlet is like the death of your kitten, you still have to determine what to do— and then *do* it. Guilt, in life or in that special part of life on the stage, is useless—what does it avail save a false sense of exemption from action?

The communists were revealed fairly early on to have created a slave state involved in mass murder. On the stage and in the studio, an addiction to confession has given rise to generations of very bad acting and generations of very bad plays. The playwrights and the actors caught it from each other. If the play contains no action (no desire of the character to achieve a goal outside of himself), then the actor need never knock it off, speak up, and get on with it. If the actors are experts schooled in self-examination (crying or bravely not crying), well, then, the writers might just as well write to their strengths.

Chekhov was a genius. His plays were not exercises in confession but were comedies, and when the characters talked about the ineffable beauty of the fireflies and so on, Chekhov was writing about the drollery of self-delusive human nature, not about the primacy of the banal.

Marlon Brando was a genius, but watching his performances we see an actor playing a character who wanted something—the quiddity of Brando came not from his deep examination of his own feelings but from his odd, essential nature as a human being. James Dean, however, was just a bad actor with a lot of nerve. To look at either and feel guilt that we are not looking deeply enough to be like them is an absurd waste of time.

Guilt is a magnificent tool for social control—enormities of the left (both abroad and at home) have been perpetrated because they invited the unconcerned first to accept a sense of guilt, and then to dispel it through magical actions. Guilt has kept generations of acting students in classes from which they will never emerge to blunder about the stage, and kept actual actors talking about their childhood in the rehearsal room until just past the last moment when it is imperative to block the play.

People come to the theatre to be delighted, amused, and shocked. To be brought to life, in short. This can never be brought about by those whose motivation is guilt, for the guilty desire to repress and deny, and the purpose of the theatre is to release and affirm. Note the prevalence of the sad dedication of this or that award by performers to some cause or other. This is a confusion. The singer, actor, or musician was honored for the ability to hit the note, sing the song, play the riff. Unsatisfied with the work itself, and with the fame or fortune it brought, he wants the additional reward of feeling guilty. And, as with the self-involved actor, he reveals not an inner worth but a profound misunderstanding of his place in the world.

THEATRICAL CULTURE

Thirty years ago I received a fellowship to teach playwriting at the Yale Drama School. My experience the first weeks suggested to me what the remainder of the year confirmed: that I could not teach playwriting.

My year-end analysis was that the rules for playwriting were few and self-evident, and to those who did not find them self-evident, that they would remain forever incomprehensible. That is to say, an interested party who could not, fairly immediately, grasp that dramatic storytelling consisted exclusively in making the audience wonder what happens next could never be brought to that understanding.*

This is not to say that the implementation of this and other basic concepts is easy; it is not. But the rule, and its few brothers, must be, to those truly inspired to learn, blatantly clear. Past the first, few simple rules, I

---

*Lately I have come to believe that acting is like writing and that both resemble swimming. The first, one would think, self-evident rule of swimming is "Don't drown."

do not believe that writing can be taught. I did believe that acting could be taught, and have spent a good deal of time over the last forty years, in my own classes and in schools and companies with which I have been associated, trying to teach acting.

Its rules are few, and, to those truly disposed to act, obvious: Speak up, turn out (find the audience, or camera), be simple. In short, as Jimmy Cagney had it, "Find your mark, look the other fellow in the eye, and tell the truth."

Someone to whom these rules are not obvious, or who is not inspired to learn to implement them, cannot act, and cannot learn to act.

A boxer has to like to fight, a surgeon to cut, and an actor to get up there and tell the story. If the actor does not yearn to do that, he may wile away decades using acting classes as a form of psychotherapy, but he will never act.

I'd suspected for some time that I actually believed the teaching of acting was bootless, but I continued teaching. Why?

(1) I enjoy it—I find it pleasant to explain and demonstrate my various theories under the ardent and perhaps dubious gaze of a roomful of students, and (2) I know of an instance where my teaching seems to have been effective.

I refer to the Atlantic Theater Company in New York. William H. Macy and I were teaching acting classes at NYU twenty-some years ago. At the end of the term, our students indicated they wanted to continue their studies, so Macy and I improvised a summer program in Vermont, and the students came north.

The program was a sort of boot camp: We rose early, did various physical things that may have included calisthenics and modern dance, proceeded to acting classes, voice classes, and I can't remember what else.

In the evening we put on plays. In subsequent years we performed live radio plays in addition to our staged offerings.

The second year the students were asked to write a book summarizing the ideas involved in the program. Six of them did (*A Practical Handbook for the Actor*), and twenty-five years later it is still in print and has sold more than a quarter of a million copies.

This year the company celebrated its twenty-fifth anniversary in New York. An outrageously large percentage of the original members are still writing, acting, directing, and producing in film, television, and onstage (the percentage of most acting students proceeding to an actual career is very, very small indeed). I once prided myself that their success could be attributed to the aesthetic ideas upon which the program was based. I don't think so anymore.

I think that one who wants to act will act, and one who wants to act better will learn from acting how to do so.

But how, then, to account for the healthy longevity of the Atlantic Theater Company, and its members?

I think that what Macy and I attempted to establish as an implement for the transmission of knowledge (the company culture) *was* the knowledge.

Our great contemporary philosopher Thomas Sowell writes in *Knowledge and Decisions* that knowledge and time are both costs in any transaction. (I don't know how to tune an engine; therefore I must pay a person who has invested in that knowledge. A pair of shoes may be cheaper across town at a wholesale outlet, but I must invest my irreplaceable time learning of the shop and driving there.)

Cultures, Sowell writes, develop as a means of reducing the costs (in knowledge, in time, and in anxiety) of decision making.

Submersion in a culture replaces a potentially universal array of choices with a specific model, which the individual imbibes so young and so naturally that its directives do not seem like choice at all, but merely the way things are.

Correct behavior toward one's seniors, juniors, superiors, family, enemies, friends, lovers, spouses, and so on, is fairly culturally specific.

We do not expend endless time or energy in determining what to wear on a first date or at a religious service, how to express condolence, warning, or apology, et cetera. (We may accept or reject these norms, but even in rejection, they are clear; the burning of a flag is an irrefutable acknowledgment of its importance as a cultural symbol.)

Macy and I, being young and enthusiastic, delighted in pushing ourselves and our students toward greater heights of dedication, which is to say, of work.

The evolved lessons of that culture included: Be prepared, be early, never complain, help your fellows, figure it out—your capacity for work is vastly greater than you suppose. Those who found those lessons taxing or uninteresting, went home; those who found them exhilarating, stayed on.

THIRD PARTIES

The life of the dramatist may seem like progress in a meritocracy, that is, in a hierarchical system where superiors award accomplishment according to a predetermined structure. But it is nothing of the kind. It is the unmonitored interaction of potential parties to a transaction.

Neither party may or can express its desires save through the unfettered operation of the free market. (Test groups claim to monitor audience desire, but films testing well fail; writers possessing many prizes and endorsements fail to capture an audience.)

The audience cannot explain "what it means" because it doesn't "mean" anything. The audience knows when its desires are met even though it cannot *say* what those desires were or are.

The playwright may express his intentions, but no one cares—except those involved in the aforementioned hierarchical system: teachers, coaches, and those

who would like to attest to the existence of this hierarchical system (critics). A minor exception is state-
supported theatre (in totalitarian regimes) and its
simulacrum (more benign but nonetheless congruent),
the subscription series.

Let us examine what happens in a playwriting/
screenwriting class. One first must gain admittance.
How does one do so? By demonstrating the ability to
attract and please an audience? No. If one could so
demonstrate, why would he seek further instruction?
The successful applicant presents credentials (academic
experience, prizes, scores on ad hoc admissions tests)
and/or something deemed by judges to be talent or
potential.

But please note that however benevolent, wise, and
foreseeing these judges may be, they can judge only
according to their particular wisdom. They cannot
judge as the audience, for they are not the audience
but individuals—in effect, critics, and, worse, critics
on a committee who must be prepared to defend
their choices logically, and to bargain and trade with
those defending their *own* prejudices—intellectuals,
the opposite, in short, of an audience. This hierarchy
cannot know the audience's desire. The artist must
learn to appeal to it.

What of his good ideas? They count for nothing.

What of his political stance and his do-gooderism? They count for less, as they are an affront to the audience that came to see a play. What of his wonderful insight? To which I respond, have you ever spent an evening with a continually insightful person? What could be more tedious?

The playwright, screenwriter, dramatist must learn to appeal to the audience. How may he do this? By observing what the audience wants. This must be done in an atmosphere unfettered by preconceptions. That is to say, in the real world: where judgment is swift and positive, unmistakable and without appeal.

This audience must be a paying audience. It doesn't matter if it's two hundred bucks for a Broadway ticket or fifty cents to see your work in a garage, they must pay something. Why?

Because then they are self-empowered to judge (the tragedy of testing is that it operates in ignorance of the free-trade nature of the theatrical exchange). The audience has paid for the right to judge, harshly and unfettered by logic or politics or worldview. "It stinks." "I loved it." These are the reactions of an audience. The tester supplants the original playwright-audience inter-action by paying—by in effect suborning—the audi-ence with a higher good, a bribe: Forgo your right to unarticulated, enjoyable judgment, and I will elect you superior to the process and very smart—in effect, you can be a critic.

Is there *anything* to be learned in the academy? Perhaps. Perhaps one might learn from observation of the difference between the actual reactions of the audience during the play and their articulated reasoning as peers or teachers afterward. But this might call for a level of sophistication obtainable only through understanding of the true, unfettered (free-market) process. (Those of you who take acting classes probably learn little from doing your scenes in front of the class but may learn something from observing the others as they work.)

The dramatist has to attract helpers, actors, funds—not from those disposed toward him through previous determination of his political, social, academic, et cetera, excellences (in effect, intellectuals, those in loco parentis) but from those with no interest whatever in his own success. But interest in their own.*

This is the essence of the theatrical interchange, and here we see that the theatre is the perfect example of the unfettered operation of a free market. The playwright gets no chance to explain to actor, investor, audi-

---

*One might enquire of the academics awarding prizes to their students for undoubted dramatic success, "Now will you invest in its commercial production?" with foreseeable results.

ence, "Here's what I meant." He can only offer his goods for sale and see if anyone buys. (Incidentally, the opinions of those who reject him, the actors and producers and directors, must be highly suspect, if not discarded outright. Why? Because—and here I am speaking of show business rather than art, anything past "no" is a waste of your time; *and* [this in the realm of how-to] each rejector will have his own hobbyhorse, his own good ideas; and in soliciting his reasons past "no" you commit the error of testing. You raise him from a legitimate potential trading partner [invited to say "yes" or "no"] and allow him to pontificate at no cost—an opportunity that few would pass up.)

What about the opinion of the audience? Its unfettered opinion must be considered, as it is the pool of potential buyers, and though you may disagree with the rejection, you must come to understand it, or starve. The audience's unarticulated rejection is the best study tool—perhaps the only study tool—of the aspiring dramatist. We know why the audience accepted this or that play or part: It was funny, it was sad, it was dramatic. But why did it, case by case, scene or beat by scene or beat, reject it?

Generally for one reason and one reason only: It was not dramatic. (Note that the teacher, the critic, the intellectual may praise or reject this or that part in an effort to keep the student, to settle a grudge, or to promote or endorse his own philosophy, but the unbribed audience has no ulterior motive. It accepts or rejects the drama, generally, to the extent that it is dramatic.)

Now what does this mean? One thing: The task of the playwright is to make the audience wonder what is going to happen next. That's it.

To say that something is dramatic means, "The piece made me want to stay on to discover what happens next."

The observant will learn (and the speed of this education will be tied directly to the dramatist's need of the audience to pay his rent) that when the audience is involved in wanting to know what happens next, it comes alive. When it no longer cares (this usually because the playwright is expounding his good ideas or great lines or scenes), the play is, in effect, over.

For the audience sits down not only willing but also *determined* to have a good time, and a good time means "wanting to know what happens next." Period. No matter what the audience or those claiming (falsely) to be its representatives (critics) may say.

The observant merchant—the dramatist—may learn from the only school where he *can* learn: in the back of the house, watching the paying audience watch his play. That is the only venue that can cure him of any unfortunate good ideas about the purpose of theatre. Whatever the purpose of theatre, it cannot achieve that purpose save through the approbation of the audience. Unless the process has been corrupted and is under the sway of intellectuals, that is, those who would impose their superior ideas on the unlettered.

In truth, then, one might reason that the only purpose of drama is to entertain the audience. And one would be correct.

How does one entertain the audience? How does one make it wonder what happens next? How does one accomplish that? Through the structuring of a plot.

That is what drama is, and that is the task of the dramatist. The plot, the structure of incidents, is all the audience cares about. The audience may not be able to articulate it, but honest (which is to say, personally necessary) observation by the dramatist will reveal this to be true. (Consider the sales-pitch meeting: When the other fellow's eyes glaze over, the meeting is done, you didn't make that sale.)

You or I may think, "But what of my talent, my ideas? What of my characters?" and so on, but stand in the back of the house and watch the first audience member yawn (let alone walk out), and learn a lesson. The task of the dramatist is the construction of a plot. Some will write snappier dialogue. Fine. Note that we enjoy plays in translation, where we have no idea how snappy the dialogue was in the original. Why do we love *An Enemy of the People*? Because of the plot.

In the back of the house (and only there), watching one's beloved play fail in front of that group that paid to see it succeed, one will learn of the importance of a plot.

How does one learn to structure, that is, to create a plot?

Read Aristotle's *Poetics*.

There we find that a plot is the necessary structure of the incidents (that is, scenes), the failure of each scene driving the hero on toward a new attempt at the solution of the goal stated at the play's outset.

There is a plague on Thebes. Oedipus, the king, sets out to find its cause. He discovers, at the end, that he is the cause. The play is over. Note that it ends in a way, as per Aristotle, both surprising and inevitable. Why has the play survived thousands of years and why did Aristotle adopt it as a paradigm? Because of its perfect plot. What must the contemporary dramatist do? Learn how to write a plot.

How is it done? By writing, revising, staging, revising, and starting again. Good luck.

ON THE GENERAL
USELESSNESS OF THE
REHEARSAL PROCESS

Prior to the late nineteenth century, plays were not rehearsed in any sense we would recognize today.

The company was directed, by the lead actor, to take up secondary places on stage and to speak and move in that fashion and to that place which would not distract from the star (e.g., contemporary opera). Stanislavsky reported that he was introduced by the Meinengen Players, sometime in the 1880s, to a different conception of staging.

Here, each player, his role large or small, was considered an equal part of a naturalistic unfolding of a human story. Stanislavsky applied this revelation, notably, to the gang comedies of Chekhov, to which form this vision is uniquely suited.

He, as director, investigated, as did the author, the psychology of the characters, giving to each the presumption of a human motive and endeavoring to communicate this to the actor. Stanislavsky, in effect, considered the character, and thus the actor, as one might consider a character in a novel: possessed of boundless, wonderful humanity, and thus capable of endless investigation.

Stanislavsky's famed (if essentially hypothetical) system, then, was and is the dissection of the motives and emotions of the character. One hundred years of actors have wasted their time in this pointless pursuit.

Why was the time a waste? The character the actor portrays is not a character in a novel, about whom we are told this or that salient fact and who, our interest piqued, may induce us to fantasize about motivation. No, the character in the play is an illusion fostered by the physical presence of the actor saying the few lines given him by the author. There is nothing else. One cannot determine where the character might have gone to school, as the character did not *go* to school.

It's just black marks on a white page.

The character *might* have been to a Laundromat just prior to coming to the stage, but there is no character, and there is no Laundromat. There are just the marks on the page and an actual flesh-and-blood human being onstage reciting them.

The character might arguably be worked up into a state of frenzy, remorse, pity, rage, or love, but the actor need no more be in that supposed state than need an opera singer. An actually suffocating opera singer would be hard-pressed to sing *Aida*. We go to the opera to hear the music, not to witness the shenanigans of the leads.

The actors, as was known of old, need merely show up and say the words in a manner to achieve a result something like that indicated by the author, and the audience will get the idea. If the audience gets the idea, the actor has not only done his job, he has done it as well as it can be done.

Why?

The audience did not come to see the actor emote, let alone pretend to emote. The playwright, to the limit of his talent and ability, removed everything from the play that was not the plot. All nicety, characterization, explanation, emotion, history, and so on, are the mark of the amateur playwright.

The great play consists of those words said by the protagonist(s) in an attempt to achieve the one goal, the announcement of which gave rise to the play. For the actor/director to glop up the play by inserting the funny, emotional, idiosyncratic, or interesting ways the actor accomplishes this goal is to undo the work of the playwright.

Why has the playwright stripped a fat story down into a lean plot? He knows this is the only way to keep the audience's interest. The audience concentrates on the stage only to discover what happens next to the hero in pursuit of his stated goal.

Why has the actor/director attempted to reinvent the wheel, by turning a plot back into a story? Because he does not understand the essence of the theatrical interchange: Cut away all embellishment and make the audience wonder what happens next.

The better the play, the easier it is to stage. Why? A good play is clear. It is clear who wants what from whom. Knowing this, the director can merely stage the actors such that, scene by scene, their intentions are clear to the audience. Let the actor learn his lines and open the damn thing.

There is no necessity to investigate the character's supposed motivations or feelings. Why? (1) They do not exist, and (2) the audience will figure them out, to the extent necessary, from the text as performed.

Why, then, these weeks of endless sitting around the table? (Note, when the time comes to actually stage the play—that is, decide who is up- and who downstage of the couch—the work will accelerate into a couple of afternoons.)

The answer dates to Stanislavsky and the unfortunate coevality of his supposed system and the work of Freud. Just as underdeprived burghers in Vienna at the turn of the century enlivened their afternoons by lying back and talking about themselves and their fantasies, so actors in Moscow and, thence, the world have beguiled their leisure hours for the last hundred years talking about themselves and the play.

Rehearsal, as generally practiced in the West, is an addictive form of group therapy and, as such, may be understood as, "I'll listen to your boring self-interested blather for a while because, in return you are honor bound to listen to mine." One may discuss endlessly the actual buying power of a ducat in fourteenth-century Venice. It won't help one play Bassanio in the least, but it is pleasant to hear oneself talk.

Lee Strasberg, Sanford Meisner, Uta Hagen, Herbert Berghof, and Stella Adler were, in various degrees of consanguinity, children of the Group Theatre, which was the first American locus of the "teachings" of Stanislavsky.

The Actors Studio (Strasberg) and the Neighborhood Playhouse (Meisner) each taught (and, supposedly, the current placeholders still teach) an essentially psychoanalytic understanding of acting, which, like psychoanalysis, focuses the attention on the self. But who wants to see a self-absorbed artist? No one. Why, then, do these schools persist?

They, like the naturalistic rehearsal process, are

addictive, as above, and they are a form of totemism. Actors and directors indulge in them as they know no better.

They forget that, at the end of the three weeks of conversation, they will actually get up, stage the play, and let the people come; and they lack the insight to eliminate the prodromal period.

There is another aspect of the tradition of rehearsal as waste: mutual confession.

The 1930s American theatre, and especially the Group Theatre and its cousin, the New Deal's Federal Theatre Project, were taken to a large extent with the myth of the Soviet miracle. Many of the members of the avant-garde were communist, or communist sympathizers. (Stanislavsky's theatre itself, of course, after the revolution flourished under communist rule.)

An essential aspect of the American Communist Party was group confession. ("Ross, the accused, sat alone at a table in the front of the hall, his face distraught. I felt sorry for him; yet I could not escape feeling that he enjoyed this." Richard Wright, in *The God That Failed*, describing the confession of an insufficiently diligent party member.)

(I remember these sessions, depoliticized, in the 1960s and renamed encounter groups.)

Here, as in the so-called Method, the operative

notion is that the human being (or his performance) is infinitely perfectible, given the courage to go deeper: If the actor can bring himself to actually *cry* (either over the death of his kitten or over his insufficiently collectivist tendencies) he has become more acceptable to the group (the jury of his peers, the audience). But the analysand interested in actually improving his state must ask not, "How did I get this way?" but, "What am I going to do about it?" For no possible answer to the first question affects the necessity of the second.

The actor actually interested in performance similarly need pay no attention to "How did the character get this way?" (What did he have for lunch? Where did he go to school?) but need only ask, "What am I going to do about it?" which is to say, "What is the character trying to bring about?" ("Why is he speaking?" rather than "What is he feeling?")

The answer to the first can be arrived at by simple analysis and need involve no emotion or in-depth analysis. Having answered this question, the director or, indeed, the actors, can quickly block the scene and put on the play.

Any other use of rehearsal time is an addiction to waste.

THE FALLACY OF
THE DIRECTOR

I have been going to the theatre for fifty years. I have seen many good and a not inconsiderable number of great performances. I have not seen that many plays well directed.

Why?

Consider: A theatrical experience (happenings, mixed media, performance art, and other such non-sense to one side) is essentially the performance of a plot, which is to say, of a story of the hero. If the story is compelling, we'll listen: The play is just a special case of the story around the campfire, or the bedtime story. Dad or Mom may not have a lovely voice, but the child will follow and enjoy the story of the Three Bears even though it is predictable and even though he has heard it before.

The plot engrosses the audience and can do so irrespective of its power to surprise.

A theatrical experience needs a text, the text needs

a plot, and the audience will pay attention even if the play is performed badly. We know there is real enjoyment, by the audience, of the revelation that the play is essentially a human story, and that, as humans, the audience is entitled to it, irrespective of how well it is performed. A theatrical experience needs a text. And it needs actors to perform it. These actors may be uniformly good or bad, or their ability may vary actor to actor.

Nonetheless, we may enjoy the play irrespective of the actors' merits. (If the play is rolling along, and we are wondering what happens next, we will forgive lack of ability in any one actor or by the actor in any one scene.)

We may reflect that when we say the actor was brilliant in the third scene, it implies that he was other than brilliant in the scenes not mentioned—he may have been merely good. But the point is that we will accept unevenness in a performance and still enjoy ourselves. For we realize the play cannot be performed without the actor.

We need a text and we need actors.

What else do we require?

Sets and costumes? Actually not.

A good play can be performed not only on a bare stage but also on the radio. This, indeed, is the test of a good play. Do we follow it absent any visual trickery?

The Fallacy of the Director

For though a set may rarely, but nonetheless ideally, improve the audience's enjoyment over that possible with a bare stage, this is the exception. Most sets exist to illustrate some idea of the designer or director the excision of which would not decrease the audience's enjoyment. The test, indeed, of a good set is: Is it better than the bare stage? The same may be said of costumes: Are they better than street clothes? The answer—theoretically, ideally—may be yes, but in the event it is usually no. And yet the audience may enjoy a production that fails these tests. (The exception is that set which does tricks, falls apart, or transforms itself in an interesting way. Any set that makes us go "ohh" is ruining the play.)

To return: Is the director needed?

No.

How do we know? First, all professionals have had the experience of staging a play without a director, in summer stock, in acting class, et cetera. And the result, most would agree, was by no means generally inferior to the norm of a directed play.

Second, all professionals have had (unfortunately frequently) the experience of a rehearsal process, I will not say directed, but moderated by a person who had no idea whatever what he was doing. And the play somehow got on in spite of it.

(An emigrant from Europe came over on a ship as a

THEATRE

child. He stood by the railing at the bow, and as the ship rose and fell, he pulled up or pushed down on the rail and, after a while, came to the enjoyable feeling that his exertions on the railing caused the up-and-down motion of a ship. So with most directors.)

What, in our experience, do most directors do during the rehearsal process? They revert to the academic or the totalitarian mode. The academic mode is this: to transform oneself into a professor teaching about the times and the themes of the play.

How does or can this inform the actor's performance? It cannot. It can only delude him into thinking that the three weeks he spends in discussion are going to do so. What happens as the play nears exposure to the audience? One, screaming, and two, *sauve qui peut*, or every man for himself.

The second mode is totalitarian.

We inherited from the Soviets and their satellites the totalitarian conception of the theatre (e.g., Brecht). That is: The theatre exists not to give the audience a good time (whether tragedy, drama, comedy, or farce) through the unfolding of a plot, but to teach or reinforce various universal but nonetheless understressed truths. These truths are usually based on the intellectual assumption that one set of humans is good and another bad: workers good, capitalists bad; women good, men bad; the afflicted good, the whole bad; gay good, straight bad.

Please note that were the paradigm inverted (straight good, gay bad), the monstrosity of the proposition would be revealed.

This notion of the betterment of humankind by intellectuals is the opposite of show business. It cannot flourish in the free market that is the essence of the human interchange, where an audience assents to pay for the experience of entertainment; it can flourish only where the audience, through ideological bludgeoning or guilt, is offered it as a substitute for entertainment.

Why would any sane person make, and any self-interested person accept, such an offer? For lack of better.

The totalitarian societies of the East and the Soviet era used the theatre as a tool of thought control. As these programs—communism, socialism, or for that matter fascism—could not stand rational analysis, the state theatres from the twenties on offered, essentially, happenings and son et lumières onto which the audience was invited to ascribe meaning. Note the spectacle of the enlightened running around Central Park clothing the trees in plastic and calling it "art," and themselves the collaborators and colleagues of Christo—the reductio ad absurdam of constructivist theatre.

An offshoot was the supposed opposition of the brave directors to the bourgeois notion of "a play" and their courage in inviting a dissatisfied audience to intuit anti-state ideas into an empty dance.*

These pro-state and anti-state constructivist presentations, however, are equally tools of totalitarianism, for they reject the primacy of the text. That is, they neither can nor will state, succinctly, the ideas contained in the performance, as such a statement would reveal the ideas either to be lacking, fatuous, or abhorrent to the audience. In these theatres—overseas and, sadly, over here—the director became primary (again, Brecht, Richard Foreman, Livio Ciuli, Andrei Serban) for it was now he, not the author, who gave meaning to the play. And as these directors could not write, they rejected the traditional dramatic text as mechanistic (Stalinist for comprehensible).

They were left with the manipulation of the plastic elements: the sets, the costumes, the lights, and masses of performers.

They were allowed to do so as they were funded by the state, and had, as Paul Johnson wrote in *Intellectu-*

---

*The audience left and leaves these agitprop spectacles self-suggested into believing the cause of their unrest is their newfound consciousness of social injustice. In fact, they are (rightly) disturbed because they have just been manipulated.

als, vast funds, unavailable to free-market theatres in the West, to rehearse indefinitely, to employ without regard to cost, and so on.

This notion of the director as prime-mover came to the West in two forms. The more benign was the setting of the play. Here beginning in the 1950s, we see lauded the bold aperçu that *Hamlet* need not be set in Denmark but may be set in Indiana.

Indeed, most directors in the West to this day are judged and perhaps applauded by critics based upon where or how they have set the play. What does it mean? That people are the same everywhere? All right. But is that worth a credit? I don't think so.

That there are similarities between Indiana and Elsinore? Again all right. But what are they? Note that the director partakes of the totalitarian in allowing us to infer a meaning that is neither present nor articulable.

For in fact *Hamlet* did not take place at Elsinore. It took place, then and now, upon a stage. For what do we know of Elsinore? Nothing. The name is a convention.

The more benign directorial impertinence is "Where do you set it?" (Similarly: Let's have some men's parts played by women, and vice versa. All right. And then what?) (A handy definition of modern art, as opposed to Art, is any production in no wise superior to a mere enumeration of the ideas contained.)

The more immediately pernicious of the directorial depredations is the denigration of the text, that is, the assertion that the text has no meaning or, at best, has only the meaning the director chooses to imbue it with.

Stanislavsky said, "Any director who has to do something interesting with the text does not understand the text." Today the problem is worse: not that the director may be ignorant of the theatrical interchange, but that he may indeed reject it in favor of some greater good—the ultima ratio of liberalism.

So we see that the director might do nothing, and the director might do harm. Might the director do good?

Yes.

We have all seen well-directed productions and may even have participated in them. What do we mean when we say that they were well directed? (Let us note that, usually, this is a second thought, following, "Golly, I enjoyed that." Why?) We probably mean that the play was clear, usually fast paced, well blocked, and well-spoken. Period.

When we leave the play saying how spectacular the sets or costumes were, or how interesting the ideas, it means we had a bad time. The director is not primary in the theatre. His job could, indeed, be disposed of.

What might he do to make the play more enjoyable

for the audience? He might help the actors to understand mechanically, scene by scene, what the characters actually want; and he might place and move them to make these relationships clearer to the audience.

That's it. If he finds or works with a brilliant designer now and then, that is, one whose work makes the play more understandable and more enjoyable to the audience than it would be absent his efforts, he is a lucky director indeed.

Learning to act is, essentially, learning to direct oneself. Learning to act is learning to ask, "What is the scene about?" and to answer that question technically and in such a way that it can be acted upon. (1) What is the character doing? (2) What does that mean in the scene? and the simple reminder, (3) What's that like to me?

Learning to act is learning to direct, to devote oneself to these simple questions exclusively—to train oneself to reject the delicious possibilities of discussion of the character and of the theme (these concerns recapsulate those of the bad director).

"Get on with it" is the task of the actor and the director. "It" in this case is bringing the play as clearly as possible to people who paid you the compliment of supposing you could entertain them.

DIRECTING FOR THE STAGE

I grew up reading a lot of theoretical books on stage-craft. I devoured everything written by and about Constantin Stanislavsky. I gobbled up the books by his protégés Vakhtangov and Meyerhold, and later by their students and devotees.

Books on directing by Tovstonogov, Nemirovich-Danchenko, and the rest of the Reds had me burning the midnight oil, nodding in grateful appreciation, and marking up the margins. I read Brecht's theoretical writings on the alienation effect, Robert Lewis, and a host of Americans on the correct implementation of the Stanislavsky system, Artaud's Theater of Cruelty, Grotowski's *Towards a Poor Theatre*, and blah blah blah.

It took me many years as a director to acknowledge that not only did I have no idea what the above were talking about, but that, most probably, they didn't either.

Stanislavsky's trilogy is a bunch of useless gack.

Brecht's gibberish about the alienation effect is, as proved by a lot of Joe Papp's oeuvre in the seventies, unimplementable.

So let's start over.

What, I reasoned, did these fellows have in common? They were all successful directors. What did that mean? They had the ability to stage a play such that the performances of the actors and the nature of the set conveyed the play's meaning to an audience sufficiently grateful to keep coming back.

As a kid playwright I watched various directors moving little cardboard cutouts representing actors around in a cardboard model of a set. This seemed to me a great idea, and when I started directing, I tried it myself, and castigated myself for what I considered a lack of discipline, when I couldn't keep my mind on the task. But, after some forty years' experience, here's what I think: The good director (and I must include all those mentioned above, as, though I never saw their work, the audiences that did indulged them for a length of time sufficient to allow them the leisure to turn theoretical) has the ability to recognize and improve spatial relationships between the actors so as to maximize, beat by beat, the play's potential for the audience.

What does this mean? There is an actual, shimmering aura or some flipping thing that exists between two actors onstage, each of whom wants something from the other. If one is aware, or gifted, or practiced, it can be felt. Your suggestion, "Oh, bushwah," might be stilled by your memory of a prizefight. Here we are very aware that the physical relationship of the fighters, after they break, tells a rather compelling story: how far apart they are, who is circling whom, are they employing the angles to evade, to lull, to prepare, to rest, et cetera.

The actors onstage, likewise, will employ their spatial relationship to affect their objectives (to get what they want from one another). Now: Most directors arrange the actors, beat by beat, scene by scene, according either to some notion of pictoriality, that is, placing them so they look pretty, or according to some predetermined, logical pattern, perhaps worked out with cardboard models.

But no, no, no. The actors must stand, and move to achieve their objective scene by scene (just as must the boxers).* When they do so, the audience's unconscious understanding of the play and, thus, enjoyment of the play are increased. This is why most plays are

---

*The actors must want something *from one another*. The nature of that desire may be better understood by the director watching the interaction of actual human beings—it can't be learned by watching pieces of cardboard.

better understood when they have not had a director.

Throw some actors into summer stock and tell them to learn the lines as the play's to go up in two nights, and their natural self-direction will be superior to most of the plays that have been graced with the services of a director. (The same, of course, is true of extras on a movie set. If one watches the small groups they naturally form themselves into while waiting for the shot to be set up, one observes a crowd scene more natural and compelling than most confected efforts. Why? Because the extras, before the camera is turned on, are forming themselves into groups and positions from which they hope to gain a simple human need: gossip, protection, companionship, shelter, information, et cetera.)

So that's one thing I know about directing: Blocking is not extraneous to but is the essence of the whole thing. The characters in the play—the actors onstage— should actually use their bodies to get what they want (just as everyone does offstage).

Older directors, that is, directors who learned to direct in front of an audience, understood this. Here's how I know.

Few who come to stage direction from TV or films, or sprang full-blown from Zeus's head, know that the actors know to move. Contemporary stage directors raised on or in film or TV will, almost invariably, place the antagonists nose to nose facing each other on a plane parallel to downstage. This means that most of the audience cannot see the faces of the actors. (See diagram 1.)

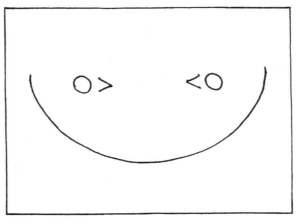

DIAGRAM 1

Previous directors did no such thing, as they realized that their rice bowl depended on the audience both seeing *and* hearing the actors. Words spoken cross stage carry out into the wings and will not be heard in the auditorium. To have the actors' words carry to the back of the house, the actor must face out.

Okay, good, now you've got the actor facing out, as in diagram 2.

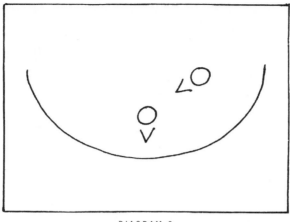

DIAGRAM 2

The upstage actor is speaking to the actor below him. We see the faces of the upstage actor speaking and the downstage actor thinking or scheming or whatever she is about.

The audience is getting the benefit of the ticket price. But hold on, the actors cannot stay in this relationship forever, can they? No. The actor downstage, "thinking" or "listening," finally makes up her mind what she is going to do, and she moves in order to do it (get the revolver, leave home). Whatever she's decided to do, she starts to move. The upstage actor says his immortal line, "Where are you going?" or whatever, and the former downstage actor has now moved upstage and turns down to deliver her response,

"I've decided to become a nurse." (See diagram 3).

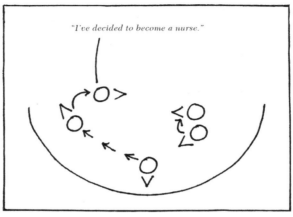

DIAGRAM 3

We note that the "natural" movement, from thinking to acting to explaining, puts the aspiring nurse
upstage, talking down to, that is, having taken the ini-
tiative from, the other actor. The balance of power
changes. Ah.

That is what blocking is all about. And that's what
the director should be doing. Additionally, he should
clarify the actions if the actors need help. (Is the aspiring nurse (a) breaking off a bad relationship? (b) taking
the first step toward a cherished goal? (c) getting out of
Dodge?)

And that is what I know about directing. I believe

most of the theoretical has been beaten out of me by decades of actors and audiences, who are the only two groups from which one may learn stage directing.

Finally, I think directing is much the same as playwriting: It's telling a story. In writing one uses words. In directing one uses people who are using words. But oh, my goodness, has it not been said that the playwright is perhaps not the best interpreter of his own works?

It probably has been said, as have most things.

But as a director, I am not interpreting my work. I'm merely staging it. Once again, in the words of Stanislavsky: "Any director who has to do something interesting with the text does not understand the text."

TIME

The great mystery in the performing arts is time. The plastic arts exist and may be contemplated at leisure. One may equally gain an impression from a momentary glance.

But the performing arts have no meaning other than that which might reveal itself over time.

Unlike painting or sculpture, they suggest, raise, and dash expectations, and eventually resolve. If they are aesthetically pleasing it is in their capacity to resolve in a way both surprising and inevitable, as Aristotle taught.

They are an exploitation of, an allusion to, and a critique of our reasoning process.

The actors, like the audience, can be told only so much.

Both have suspended reason in favor of experiment and adventure. The director must say very little to the actor, and that little must be capable of being acted upon ("Cross the stage to here and pause" is a fulfillable direction; "Become more introspective" is not).

When the actor's eyes light up, or he nods, or he has any physical reaction to the direction, it is time for the director to shut up; the actor is indicating that he wants to *act*. Any information past this point is convincing him otherwise. There is only so much information an actor can assimilate in the course of the day, so the director must hold his tongue and stringently monitor his desire to express himself; for when the actor runs out of attention the rehearsal is done.

The audience's attention, similarly, is limited. To tell in a line, a scene, an act more than the audience members can act upon will force them to use their reason. (A playground game: The children explaining the rules naturally keep them simple, for their aim is to tell the newcomers only enough to allow all—old and new—to get on with the game. And have some fun. If the brief explanation before the schoolyard game becomes the Paris peace talks, then the game is no longer worth the candle.)

(My family sat down to play a board game. We opened the package and began reading the rules. They seemed taxing and interminable. Then my wife remembered she had played this game as a child and told us, in two sentences, the logical and clear rules that would allow us to play.)

The author and director are, to the audience, in the same position as the leader of the new game.

Our goal must be to say as quickly and simply as possible only those rules that allow all to participate.

What is the purpose of the rules? To balance difficulty with ambition, in order to allow the dramatic urge to function. The playhouse here is the same as the schoolyard: The rules of both are to allow for drama.

The kids in the schoolyard have a limited amount of attention. They have gathered at the promise of adventure and will listen to the rules as long as they see them as aids to that end.

The plot, similarly, is a brief explanation of the rules of the game, of such compactness and integrity that if even one element were taken away, the play would be incomprehensible.

The mystery in drama is time: how to use time, how to exploit the human perception of time and its ordering into cause and effect. The rejection of this intolerable burden, our human specialty, is the goal of the religious mystic, the yogi, the lover, and the drug addict—to live in a world without time, to achieve unbeing.

The examination of this urge and its avowal and the confession of its tragic impossibility is the subject of all drama.

ACKNOWLEDGMENTS

I am very much indebted to the works of Thomas Sowell, Paul Johnson, Frederich Hayek, and Milton Friedman, and to those of Richard Wright and Eric Hoffer.